Sacred Time and the Search for Meaning

Sacred Time

AND THE

Search for Meaning

GARY EBERLE

Shambhala

BOSTON & LONDON

2003

Shambhala Publications, Inc.
Horticultural Hall
300 Massachusetts Avenue
Boston, Massachusetts 02115
www.shambhala.com

9 8 7 6 5 4 3 2 1

First Edition

Printed in the United States of America

❦ This edition is printed on acid-free paper that meets the American
National Standards Institute Z39.48 Standard.

Distributed in the United States by Random House, Inc.
and in Canada by Random House of Canada Ltd.

Library of Congress Cataloging-in-Publication Data
Eberle, Gary.
Sacred time and the search for meaning/Gary Eberle.—1st ed.
p.   cm.
Includes bibliographical references.
ISBN 1-57062-962-5 (alk. paper)
1. Time—Religious aspects. 2. Sabbath. I. Title.
BL65.T55 E24 2003
291.3'6—dc21
2002008068

For Sue and Will

Contents

ACKNOWLEDGMENTS

THANKS TO AQUINAS COLLEGE for the gift of time in the form of a sabbatical leave to begin this work. Thanks to Kim Kenward and Jeanine Weber for help with interlibrary loan and for teaching me the finer points of electronic research. Thanks to Rabbi Albert Lewis, Rev. Bruce Bode, Fr. Dan Davis O.P., Sr. Mary Navarre O.P., Miriam Pederson, and Pamela Waterbury for their helpful reading of drafts of some chapters of this book. Thanks to Mary Hietbrink, whose editorial suggestions helped me find a clear focus for the book. Thanks to Marianne Graff for help with Latin translations. Special thanks to Rob Beahan for use of the cabin that time forgot, and to my editor, Emily Bower. And, as always, big thanks to Sue and Will Eberle, who understood my need for time to complete this book.

Introduction

WHEN I BEGAN RESEARCHING and writing this book, I was more than usually concerned with questions of time and how it passes.

Like many people in midlife, I found myself burdened with multiple responsibilities to my job, family, and community. In spite of good intentions, I never seemed to have enough time to devote to any of them. I found myself spread thin, and the many supposedly time-saving gadgets of the modern world (computers, answering and fax machines, microwave ovens, e-mail) did not help. Every moment was overfilled, and there never seemed to be enough time to do the things I had to do, much less the things I wanted to do.

It was not a question of "time management." I knew all the usual tricks. Not only had I taken time management workshops, I had actually taught them. I was clustering my phone calls and e-mail, handling papers only once, using all the most efficient technology, yet I still could not keep up with the flow. I needed a thirty-hour day.

What was happening? Was I just getting older? Is survival in this hyperspeed world a younger person's game, I wondered, or is there something about the way we live today that is significantly different from the way people lived in the past? Why is it that there seems to be no breathing space anymore?

With these questions in mind, I started working on this project. It was shortly after my forty-fifth birthday. This was a significant time for me because my father had died quite suddenly just before his own forty-fifth birthday. I realized I had grown older than my father. That was oddly unsettling. The rattling of "time's winged chariot" seemed somehow more insistent; thoughts of death and immortality and questions of ultimate meaning pressed themselves on me. I realized that for a long while I had not thought about these things. Why? Like everyone else, I simply had not had time. The events of this world demanded attention, while eternity seemed to make no demands at all. Eternity could wait. But could it?

After writing a book about the loss of sacred space in our lives, I realized that we have lost a sense of sacred time as well. Sacred time is time devoted to the heart, to the self, to others, to eternity. Sacred time is not measured in minutes, hours, or days. Sacred time, like sacred space, is necessary to our well-being, but sacred time has grown increasingly difficult to find.

The modern world runs strictly by the clock. From the moment the alarm sounds in the morning, we are immersed in the quick flow of social time. The computers we work with all day measure our lives in nanoseconds. Bulging daily planners and personal digital assistants make sure we keep every waking second filled with activities. We are booked and double-booked from dawn until we turn off the television or shut down our home computer at night. Why this manic pace? Why do we rarely, if ever, step outside time's flow to examine the fast-paced lives we are leading? Why can't we look at our lives *sub specie aeternitatis*, from the perspective of eternity, as others have done before us?

Perhaps, I thought, we modern folk have grown afraid of those quiet times our ancestors took for granted, those moments in the dark, without external stimuli, when human beings looked inside themselves and examined the slower rhythms of their existence. That has always been the path to wisdom, but we seem to have abandoned it in recent years. Or at least we seem to have lost the time needed to follow that road.

Then I began to wonder what happens to us, individually and as a society, when we cease to visit those "eternal" places within ourselves on a regular basis. The answer, of course, quickly became clear. We end up with the frantic, fragmented, fast-paced life we experience on the commercial strip or read about in the daily news or log on to in cyberspace. It is a world without permanence, a world in which the only constant is change, a world untouched by anything we might call eternity. Yet, without regularly touching eternity, we live in a world without cohesion and depth, a world in which "time flies" in an ever-accelerating rhythm until we want to shout, in the words of the old Broadway show title, "Stop the World, I Want to Get Off!"

I seemed to understand the problem, but there seemed to be no way to solve it. The momentum of the world around me seemed too great. The Sabbath, a regular day of rest, had disappeared as a cultural institution from the secular world I lived in. We let it slip from our fingers sometime in the past thirty years or so. Our hurry-up, twenty-four-hour-a-day lives will not allow Sabbaths, or spiritual resting places, and so time seems to fly ever faster, and we constantly feel we have less and less of it. A permanent sense of lost or wasted time seems to haunt us, no matter how successful we are. "If only I had the time" becomes a constant refrain.

Ironically, this sense of being hungry for more time comes in an age when we live longer than humans ever have, in a time when we pride ourselves on our time-saving devices. Yet we are scant of breath and pant for more time. Surprisingly, we don't find this phenomenon in, say, the European Middle Ages. Then the vast majority of people had short and uncomfortable lives, yet they seemed to luxuriate in time and to maintain the capacity for celebrating life's abundance, for they believed that this brief bodily existence was but a fraction of an eternal life possessed by every living creature. Where and when did we lose our sense of participation in endless, sacred time? Can that sense be got back again in the midst of our machine-made, speed-mad world?

As all of these questions buzzed in my head, I decided to take advantage of the academic tradition of the sabbatical, a time out of time, based on the Hebrew Scriptures' recommendation of a fallow period every seven years to allow the fields to return to fertility. For one year I let go of my responsibilities at Aquinas College, where I have taught literature and humanities for over twenty years. For a full year, I endured the taunts of my jealous colleagues and neighbors who accused me of being on vacation or just plain lazy. I traveled to Italy for a month with my wife and son, I wrote a novel and some short stories, and I read about time. I pondered works by authors both ancient and modern.

I admit there were moments of vertigo during my sabbatical year, times when I felt events were passing me by, when I feared I was falling behind in some race everyone else seemed to be running. Gradually, however, I got used to my newer, slower rhythm. During my so-called fallow year, I wrote, I read, I reflected. I returned to a meditation practice I had never completely abandoned but had "not had time for" for several years. I pondered my Catholic upbringing, and, in Rome and Ravenna, I meditated on the history of fallen empires. For the first time in a long time, I lived with an eye regularly turned toward eternity.

As my sabbatical drew to a close, I wrote much of the first draft of this book as a way of preserving for myself a reminder that the hectic stream of time I was about to reenter was not the only way to be. As I began my research and reflection, it seemed that sacred time was the great white whale of topics. It was everywhere and nowhere, monstrous and uncatchable, but always tantalizing and tempting one further. Gradually, I realized that sacred time, eternity, is not remote or "out there." Rather, it is always with us. It is the steady underpinning of our lives and is always and everywhere only a thought away. Time-tested methods of prayer and meditation from many traditions exist to take us there whenever we wish. Only we have lost faith in their power to deliver us from time's quick flow.

The following pages attempt to pull together some thoughts on these questions in an age that believes it has no time to give to them. This book is partly an essay on time and partly a record of a personal journey to find, or refind, sacred time in the contemporary world. Though I have referred to the work of many scholars, this is not a scholarly tome. Rather, in the tradition of essayists like Ralph Waldo Emerson, Thomas Carlyle, Matthew Arnold, and Michel de Montaigne, it is an attempt by an educated layperson to take a point of view on a contemporary problem in a literate and, I hope, enlightening way. My method has been like Henry David

Thoreau's definition of walking: I set out to find sacred time and then let way lead on to way, rather careless of getting anywhere in particular, fiercely guarding the freedom to change routes and directions, keeping the goal always in front of me. From my initial inquiries into timekeeping and spiritual experience, I traveled from the Paleolithic era to the present, from the pre-Socratics through Augustine and on to a rereading of Pierre Teilhard de Chardin after a lapse of more than twenty years. I set aside time for Zen meditation, prayer, and participation in the liturgical year of the Catholic Church.

The result was a deepened understanding of the relationship between time and eternity. And so I ask the reader to join me in the spirit of an interesting walk or after-dinner conversation, or any of the other desultory and "sacred" activities that enrich our lives immeasurably but that we don't often take time for in our too-busy world. I can only hope that the thoughts that follow can enrich some other reader's life as the ideas and experiences recounted here have enriched mine.

Sacred Time and the Search for Meaning

CHAPTER I

No Time Like the Present

A TYPICAL MODERN FAMILY is awakened from sleep not by the gradual rising of the sun but by the abrupt blare of a clock radio. The clock's LCD shows the current time in bright numbers that illuminate the darkness. It is 6:45 A.M. The abbreviation A.M. is from the Latin *ante meridiem*, meaning that the sun has not yet hit the midpoint in its daily journey. In fact, the sun has not yet even risen above the horizon, but we don't normally notice sunrise anyway. The sun's rising doesn't matter. We run our lives by the clock alone. As the morning news comes out of the radio, we get a sense of urgency. While we slept, time marched on. Bombings occurred, governments were toppled. The situation is grave. The LCD blinks. It is 6:46. A minute has passed. Time to catch up and get moving.

In this typical household, everyone hurries in the morning. Our family has a schedule to keep, and each person's individual timetable must synchronize smoothly with everyone else's or the family's master schedule will be thrown off. If we adults are really on the ball, we have already started our workday by reading last night's e-mail on our home computer while finishing our instant breakfast. As we pull out of the driveway, we make the first phone calls of the day from our cell phone to get things set at the office. Meanwhile, the kids are meeting their bus, which is also on a tight schedule. They must get to school before the opening bell. If they miss the bell, which rings at 8:05 sharp, they will be penalized with demerits. At the same time, we are making our daily trek through what is called, for some reason, the rush hour, even though very little rushing goes on during this time and it is often longer than an hour.

During rush hour, we find ourselves tense and angry. Racing the clock, we bang on the steering wheel, honk, and make rude gestures at complete strangers. We feel we are not moving fast enough. Fast enough for what? That question rarely gets asked. The sense of urgency is compounded by the fact that we have been listening to the latest news from around the world on the TV or car radio. Things are happening, there's been a coup d'etat in a far-off country, financial markets have been open for hours somewhere in the world, and now we find ourselves behind some slowpoke going forty-five miles an hour in the express lane!

Fortunately, like our office equipment, we modern people have become good at "multitasking." Without thinking much about it, we routinely do several things at once in order to "save time." We simultaneously pack lunch for the kids, monitor the war on terrorism, read the morning e-mail, feed the dog, and tend to personal grooming without losing step. Even so, most of us begin our days feeling we are already behind. We are one day older, one day closer to death. Stalled in traffic, we make another typical modern gesture. We flick our left wrists to check the time every few minutes or, under stress, seconds. We are compulsive about this gesture. Often we look at our watches and don't even register the time. Even so, they show it to the minute and second. They are marvels of precision, these watches. Many remind us of the date and day of the week, as well as the hour and minute. Some double as stop watches, in case we need to time something in hundredths of a second. They beep on the hour, every hour. In the not-so-distant future, they may become even more important. They will contain minicomputers to hold our appointment books. They will have pulse and blood pressure monitors, miniature address files, small calculators, and satellite uplinks to worldwide weather reports.

We modern workers rely on other things besides watches to keep us on time. We carry daily planners or digital organizers to schedule our days and lead us from task to task. We purchase ever-faster machines that are supposed to make our lives more efficient and organized. We take workshops on time management that treat time as if it were a wild animal that could be cowed into submission. Thus, the day becomes a constant flow of tightly scheduled activities: morning meetings followed by business lunches followed by more meetings and more appointments in a workday that typically lasts from eight to ten hours or more.

Our children are prepared for this world by their highly regimented school day, in which bells and buzzers put limits on the time spent learning this subject or that. At most schools, a forty-five- or fifty-minute period is given to all subjects: typing, literature, woodworking shop, mathematics, and so on. Everything is made to fit into this block, except for lunch. Lunch is usually shorter, since we regard eating as little more than necessary refueling so we can keep up the pace.

At the end of their day, children and adults fly home, but things are not much better there, at least in terms of feeling they have enough time. Dinner comes out of a microwave oven, but not quickly enough. After all, a microwave takes minutes to cook supper, and in lives measured in micro- or even nanoseconds, minutes have become what hours used to be. We may find ourselves dancing nervously in front of the microwave, mumbling, "Come on, come on!"

After our fast food, we may relax by allowing our evening to be determined by the schedulers who arrange what we call "prime time" entertainment. There, in a jerky rhythm of camera shots lasting from three to thirty seconds, in story segments of six to seven minutes interrupted by several thirtysecond commercials, we are entertained by the manic, speeded-up rhythm of television. The result is entertainment that consists of short snatches of dialogue and as many one-minute emotional traumas as we can stand before flicking our attention to something else.

At the end of the day comes bedtime. Bedtime is not determined by whether or not we are tired. Most of us are usually tired enough for bed about the time darkness falls on the outside world. But we let our day's end be determined by the television schedule: either a few laughs courtesy of a late-night talk show host or one last blast of news delivered by satellite from someplace in the world where it is already tomorrow. The last act to end this manic day is setting the clock radio that will hunch in the dark like an electronic rooster until it crows us into the next hectically scheduled round.

There are, of course, weekends, those pauses between the busy workdays that we set aside in order to relax, a word that, according to the *Oxford English Dictionary*, didn't even exist in English until the 1400s (coincidentally, about the same time clocks came into being in Europe) and didn't get its current meaning of taking time from work until late in the 1700s. But, of course, when we relax (literally, loosen) on the weekends, we do it in a thoroughly modern way. If we stay home, we attack a list of household chores that we feel we have to finish as efficiently and quickly as possible. If we have a couple of days away, we cram a long string of activities into the forty-eight or so hours of "free time" we have. Loading our cars with all the stuff of our daily lives, we join the Friday night caravans out of the city to go mountain biking, rock climbing, canoeing, cross-country skiing. We go frantically from Friday until Sunday night, trying to make the most of our free time, because on Monday the alarm will ring again and we will begin the next leg of this strange race whose finish line seems to recede before us the faster we run.

Is it any wonder that in recent years doctors are seeing increasing numbers of people suffering from chronic fatigue syndrome or that virtually everyone today feels generally harried and hurried? A quick glance at the magazine rack in the supermarket shows cover stories on time management, articles that tell us how to squeeze more activities into the dwindling personal time we feel we have, or tips on how to cope with a speeded-up life that no one seems to have asked for. From the advertisement pages, beautiful models slouch and pout at us looking bored, as if they had nothing to do. That may be what they are really selling. More than fashions or cars, they are selling us leisure time. The message in ad after ad is "Buy our product and we will give you time," time to lounge on the beaches, time to luxuriate in a bubble bath, time to drive in the mountains, time to golf and play and flirt and have personal lives just like these models. But it is an illusion. To buy the products that promise us leisure, we must work harder than ever.

Increasingly, we feel we are living out those archetypal images of modernity from the silent film era: like Charlie Chaplin, we are being pulled through the gears and cogs of an assembly line faster and faster; like Harold Lloyd, we are dangling precariously from the hands of a big clock—only in these troubled times clocks no longer have faces or hands, only cold numbers.

It wasn't supposed to be this way. Fifty years ago, at the dawn of the TV and computer age, we were told that the future would be a time of relaxation and human development. Our machines would do the work and we would live in a demiparadise of leisure. But at the beginning of the twenty-first century, the values of speed and efficiency have become so much a part of our daily routine that they rule and shape our lives in ways we are not even aware of. The proverbs that guide our lives reveal our attitudes: never put off until tomorrow what you can do today; time is money; time is of the essence. We live in a state of perpetual urgency. We try to become one-minute managers, and we eat at fast food shops called Hot 'n' Now or Get 'em and Go. Things have become so bad that this manic lifestyle seems normal to us. It seems the inevitable result of progress. It even seems good for us. "Better than being bored," we say as we buy another product that is supposed to save us time, be more convenient, and make us happy in the bargain. We live by the unquestioned assumptions of our culture: faster is always better, efficiency rules.

Of course, this makes for a lopsided life. The pace cannot continue without sooner or later taking some toll. Focusing exclusively on clock time, it ignores the other time dimensions we experience in meditation and prayer, in the creative mode that psychologist Mihaly Csikszentmihalyi has called "flow state," and in contact with that time of no-time that traditionally has been called eternity. The wisdom literature of the world tells us that reaching those other states takes time, sometimes several lifetimes, and time is what we feel we don't have. So if we try to find sacred time at all, we look for quick and easy enlightenment. We seek seven fast steps to peace and calm, instant satori, as though the getting of wisdom could be subjected to a cosmic time-and-motion study and made more efficient. In the end, most of us just give up and keep moving so we don't "fall behind."

Whatever happened to sacred time? Sacred time is what we experience when we step outside the quick flow of life and luxuriate, as it were, in a realm where there is enough of everything, where we are not trying to fill a void in ourselves or the world, where we exist for a moment at both the deepest and the loftiest levels of our existence and participate in the eternal life of all that is. In simpler, or perhaps just slower, times, people seemed to enter this realm more regularly, or perhaps even to live with one foot inside it. Prayer, meditation, religious rituals, and holy days provided gateways into eternity that allowed us to return to the world of daily time refreshed and renewed, with an understanding that beneath the busyness of daily life there was an underpinning of calm, peace, and sufficiency.

Clearly something has happened to our experience of time, and sacred time in particular. We human beings are temporal creatures through and through. We're not the only creatures on the planet to tell time, of course. Nature is full of remarkable examples of creatures that have the ability to know what time it is: seventeen-year locusts, mayflies, butterflies, anadromous salmon, and the swallows that return to Capistrano all show a remarkable ability to know the correct time to mate, emerge, or migrate. Even plants like the night-blooming cereus have exquisite timing. The lives of bees and flowers are intricately synchronized. Nature provides us with no end of examples of deeply embedded timing processes in various species.

And yet the human temporal sense seems more thorough-going than these. Our timing mechanisms are more complex than simple migratory or mating switches in the brain stem, and we seem to experience time through virtually all levels of our consciousness. We are like fish swimming in a sea of time, permeated by it.

For simplicity's sake, however, let's say we have two main ways of experiencing time: horizontally and vertically. The horizontal takes us along a straight line from past to future. This is what allows us to plan events and schedule meetings. It is the time we measure with clocks. The other way of experiencing time, the vertical, seems to deliver us from the flow of horizontal time. In moments of rapture, deep meditation, dream states, or intense celebration, we feel liberated from time's passing. The clock does not stop, of course, but we do not hear it ticking. When we connect with vertical time, we step out of horizontal time and touch eternity. We might, therefore, think of ourselves as temporal amphibians, capable of living in either of these temporal modes at different times, and indeed of having to move back and forth between them as frogs move back and forth from land to water for different phases of their life cycle.

Mostly, we live in what philosopher Martin Heidegger in *Being and Time* called a "horizon of temporality."[1] Time surrounds us like the horizon that forms the perimeter of the world, and it flows in one direction only. The past is behind us and the future is before us. We are able to travel into the past through memory and to project ourselves into the future with imagination. We stand at the center in what we call the present. This "horizontal time" is what we call clock time. It is the time of appointments, shopkeeping, and work. It flows in a straight line onward. This is the time human beings "tell" with our various time-keeping devices. To do so seems a nearly universal trait with many variations.

Our ancestors in the Pleistocene age incised marks on reindeer antlers to show the passing of days between moons, perhaps to calculate hunting seasons. The Nuer people of Africa use a complicated method of reckoning time that involves memorizing complex intergenerational relationships so individuals always know precisely where they stand in history. In ancient China, time was told by the burning of an incense clock so one knew the time by the smell of the smoke in the air. In the eighteenth century, Europeans spent massive amounts of time, money, and ingenuity to develop a reliable spring-run clock to make exploration of the seas possible. Today, scientists measure time using the piezo-electric vibrations of a cesium atom and coordinate "leap seconds" to keep the complex webs of modern electronic communications intact.

The time we tell in all these ways is horizontal time. Our personal time is composed of our own memories and our aspirations for the future. Our sense of horizontal time grows more acute as we grow older. As we mature, we become aware of history, a stream of time into which we have been born. Our own memories and aspirations merge with all the traditions, stories, and memories others have passed down to us. We become aware of how we fit as individuals into the cultural institutions, rituals, kinship patterns, and general social organization that have been handed down through time. We also learn to anticipate and participate in bringing about the collective future envisioned by our society.

This collective historical past and future may be longer or

shorter depending on one's culture. For example, some primal peoples' collective concept of the past is simply the "not now." In preliterate cultures like the Australian aboriginal culture, the "deep past" may be, by our reckoning, only a few generations. It consists of the period just before anyone currently living remembers anything personally. Everything else occurred in the "dream time" of mythology, whether it happened a hundred years ago or a hundred thousand years ago—indeed, whether it ever occurred at all. The future may be tomorrow or next moon or next rainy season or simply "not now."

By contrast, people living in modern cultures have a greatly expanded and complicated time horizon to deal with. Over the past few hundred years, Western civilization and the modernized world have come to base themselves on Newtonian or "absolute" time, the belief that time is linear and each event in time happens only once in an unrepeatable sequence. This means that our time horizon, our mental time map of the world we live in, is vastly larger than that of previous generations, and this could be a part of the reason we feel the pressure of time so constantly.

In our modern understanding, the universe's past extends back some 15 billion years. This number is so awesome it may reduce our sense of the significance of our own lives, or even the life span of our species, to almost nothing. Compared to 15 billion years, even the life span of our planetary system dwarfs to insignificance.

The past for us did not used to be so long. Until the last two hundred years, the Western world's collective history was fairly short, comparable even to the mythic past of the aborigine. In the 1600s, the Irish prelate James Ussher tried to figure out the age of the world by using the Bible to add up the ages of patriarchs all the way back to the first day of Creation in Genesis. He concluded that the world was only some 5,500 years old.[2] That's not such a huge number. With relatively little effort a person in Ussher's day could hold the whole history of the universe in his or her head simply by memorizing who begat whom in the Bible. Ussher was confident that a mere thirty or so generations separated him from Adam and Eve. It must have been comforting to exist inside a time horizon that small, for all of history would have been comprehensible. The present was not far removed from the sacred time of Creation, and each individual's place in time (and eternity) was sure. To people who believe they are separated from the "dream time" of Creation by only a few generations, the world must seem fresh and new. Like Adam and Eve before the Fall, they walk with their God in the cool of the evening, or at least their near ancestors did.

Since Ussher's time, of course, the time horizon of our Western world has expanded enormously, and the task of wrapping our minds around the collective history of our species has become nearly impossible.

The expansion of historical time began in the late 1700s, with the geological discoveries of Charles Lyell. It worked its way into popular consciousness after 1859, when Charles Darwin's *Origin of Species* was published. Lyell's work on the development and age of geological strata made it clear that the universe was immensely older and more impersonal than anyone had ever thought before. Counter to people's assumption that they lived in a mental world and universe created by an omnipotent God in a mere seven days in an October some 5,500 years before them, the nineteenth-century scientists' work seemed to prove that Creation actually took place over millions of years. The British scientist William Thompson, later Lord Kelvin, stunned the Victorians in 1864 when he calculated that the earth became solid, from its molten state, at least 20 million years and perhaps as many as 400 million years earlier. As scientific theory continued to put together a clearer picture of the origins of life on earth, we had to contend with the fact that for many millions of years, there was no life on earth at all.

For Bishop Ussher, historical time and sacred time overlapped. God was there from the start and continued to act in the world. Seed-bearing plants and fruit trees came on day three, fish and birds on day four. Other mammals and humans came along on day six, and Bishop Ussher arrived only thirty generations later.

Lyell and Darwin, by contrast, showed that life on earth came about incredibly slowly. Species took millions of years to develop. And humanity, so central to the Genesis story of Creation, was a Johnny-come-lately species. According to the new time scheme, humans first evolved from apes long before Ussher's first day of Genesis, but long after dinosaurs and other species perished from the earth.[3] Scientists were showing that, paradoxically, the world began before the Bible's "in the beginning." The disturbing irony and potential threat to everything they believed was not lost on the Victorians. A Victorian bishop's wife became infamous for saying to her husband that she hoped it wasn't true, but if in fact humans *were* descended from the apes, then she prayed it would not become generally known. For better or worse, her fear came true.

Modern followers of Darwin have pushed the human time horizon even farther back. They now estimate that humans appeared, in their first form, some 4.5 million years ago. This multiplies by a factor of about 900 percent the work we have to do to hold the collective past of our species in our heads. An individual's life span, once removed by only thirty-three or thirty-four generations from the sacred origins of human-kind, is now seen to be a mere speck in a vast ocean of time, our allotted three score and ten more ephemeral than the life of a mayfly.

Today, most cosmologists accept that the universe itself is about 15 billion years old. The number is virtually incomprehensible.

Among the hallmarks of our modern life are widespread feelings of alienation and anxiety, of not feeling at home in the universe. Maybe these anxieties come at least in part from the fact that the comfortable, human-centered, and relatively young mental universe we used to inhabit has been replaced by an immeasurably older and colder mental universe, one that may not be centered on us at all. Perhaps the tremendous size of the time world we need to hold in our minds has something to do with the problems experienced by the typical modern family at the beginning of this chapter. In a world that began "in the beginning," as did the world painted for us by Genesis and other great cosmogonic myths, we feel that the present is separated from the sacred origins of life by only a few generations of human ancestors, who were present shortly after if not right at the creation of things, who even consorted with the gods in the early days. Today the world of the gods is immeasurably distant. And so, perhaps for that reason, our society has arrogantly turned its back on the past and thinks mainly about the future.

More than the present or the past, of course, the future is where most of us live today. We feel we must push ourselves into its perpetual "not yet," living for the next thing, the next moment, the one we're not in. Living in the modern world, it is impossible not to feel a kind of pressure exerted on us by the future. This pressure is in the daily planner filled with coming appointments. It is in the five-year and ten-year strategic plans we constantly update. It is in the modern anxiety that the future will come and go and we will somehow be left behind. The future is the time we are constantly trying to save and not lose or waste, and, like the past, it too has lost its connection with sacred time.

In Bishop Ussher's mythological view, the past was not that long ago, and the future coming of the end of time was imminent. In his view, history would be rounded out by the Second Coming of Jesus, and this vale of tears would be subsumed into eternity. The entire history of the universe was headed for a sacred conclusion. Time had a purpose and a direction. The view of time that has evolved since then is quite different.

Edward T. Hall, in *The Dance of Life*, says we modern, Westernized peoples think that the future comes at us like empty bottles along an unstoppable and nearly infinite conveyor belt.[4] We feel a pressure to fill these different-sized bottles (days, hours, minutes) as they pass, for if they get by us without being filled we will have wasted them. This is a strange and mechanistic view of time, quite different from other cultures' notions of the time that is "not yet." It forms what German historian Reinhart Koselleck called the "weight" of the future that presses on us to do something with our time, to make it productive, to make every minute count. We feel we must "make" the future, for it will not simply unfold according to fate or God's will. Furthermore, if we don't create this future, someone else will, and we will be left in the wake. Unfortunately, like poor Charlie on the assembly line, we also find that someone is constantly cranking up the speed. The future comes at us all too quickly, and the most we can do is pick up the pace so that not one of those time bottles gets past us without our putting at least something into it.

This attitude about time is older than America, but Americans raised it to a form of religion. In 1748, Ben Franklin, in his *Advice to a Young Tradesman*, wrote his famous adage that time is money. Franklin pointed out that if the young man could have made ten shillings in a day but went out on a lark for half the day, he actually lost five shillings by not laboring. Time spent not working is money wasted.

This attitude about the use of time is inevitably frustrating, and it probably accounts for what psychoanalyst Karen Horney early in the twentieth century called "the neurotic personality of our time." In her fascinating 1937 essay of that title, Horney claimed that while the chief pathology presenting itself to Freud and early psychiatry in the late 1800s was "hysteria," that diagnosis was no longer as common by the 1930s. The sexual repressions of the late-nineteenth-century Victorians had been thrown off in the Roaring Twenties. What replaced hysteria, in her view, was a different pathology, a constellation of neurotic behaviors that stemmed from "problems of competition, fears of failure, emotional isolation, distrust of others, and of our own selves" that had become accepted as "normal" in our society.[5] As a description of life in the twentieth century, the symptoms Horney listed are all too familiar: anxiety; hostility; the neurotic need for affection; the quest for power, prestige, and possessions; neurotic competitiveness; and compulsive sexuality as a means of seeking the affection we feel the absence of. Of course, these feelings are probably found to some degree everywhere, but Horney's point was that they somehow came into particular relief in our modern culture, and they formed the special neurotic character of our time. If any one diagnosis could be applied collectively to all these symptoms, it would be obsessive-compulsive disorder. Modern people, Horney wrote, are gripped by compulsions that mimic the machine age they live in. When people were freed from repression, even their sexual lives took on a compulsive quality. Even in Horney's time, long, leisurely sensuality was being replaced by the hurried encounter that would eventually become known as the quickie. Obsessive-compulsives must fill their time with activities, no matter how meaningless, or their world seems to fall apart.

Of course, the situation is worse today than when Horney wrote. Our whole society seems to organize itself to groom obsessive-compulsive types from the cradle up. Any activity is better than none, for we must not waste time. Increasing numbers of people seem driven by energies that are machine-like. Indeed, many people betray a strange envy of their machines. If one of the by-products of the Industrial Revolution was that human workers were devalued because they could not work as long, as hard, or as steadily as their steam-driven equipment, then one of the serious by-products of the current information revolution is that many of us have shrunk in our own estimation because we are not as fast, efficient, tireless, or "smart" as the computers we interact with every day. Computers can work and work and work. We can't.

Today, we feel the pressure of the future more insistently because the speed with which it comes at us has accelerated greatly in just the past ten years. Microcomputers working in nanoseconds set the pace. When human chess master Garry Kasparov was about to go up against IBM's Deep Blue computer in May 1997, the cover of *Newsweek* touted the game as "The Brain's Last Stand." Alas for us humans, Kasparov lost.

The speed of the present and the pressure of the future have created what Steffan Linder has eloquently called "time famine." We hunger for time to do the things we want to do at the pace we want to do them, in the order and at the time we, not some machines, determine. Our responses to time famine, however, have not been very effective. To appease our hunger for more time, we paradoxically have speeded up activities like eating, recreation, sex, and work in order to get more time. If our goal is to be able to do what we like at the pace we like and when we like, we will never achieve it that way. Nonetheless, we continue to attempt to manage time, to tame it, to use it more efficiently, but the upshot is that we hunger for it even more.

Time famine was not created by computers alone, of course, and it is not unique to the last ten years. Computers are simply the latest wave of modernism that has brought it about. We could define modernism as the complex of technological and cultural changes that have taken place since about 1880 that have resulted in life's being experienced as faster, more alienating, and more fragmented than ever before.[6]

What we call the modern mentality started emerging between 1600 and 1700 in the form of the scientific revolution and the Enlightenment and flowered around 1800 with the Industrial Revolution. By the end of the nineteenth century, it had gained momentum and caused the radical acceleration in the way people lived that today makes contemporary life move in hyperspeed. In the remarkable thirty-year period between 1880 and 1910, virtually all of the inventions that make life in the modern world recognizable came into being. Electricity was harnessed for home and industrial use, and an outpouring of inventions followed: the telephone, telegraph, record player, motion picture projector, cathode-ray tube, and many others. This era gave us the automobile and the airplane, the X ray and the radio, and it eventually led to jet airplanes, instant cameras, television, communications satellites, personal computers, and the Internet, all of which closed distances and speeded up time.

Obsolescence became a major factor in technology. As new inventions came on the scene, we had shorter and shorter intervals in which to become familiar with them before the next version or invention made the old technologies part of the rubbish heap of history. Alvin Toffler, in the 1970s, called it "future shock," and everyone recognized the symptoms in themselves. Historian Reinhart Koselleck noted that future shock or something like it is "certain to be an effect of the technical-industrial modification of a world that forces upon its inhabitants ever briefer intervals of time in which to gather new experiences and adapt to changes induced at an accelerating pace."[7]

Baby boomers are old enough to remember the promise of several waves of technology since the 1950s that were going to simplify our lives and release us from drudgery so that "in the future" human beings would have ample leisure time to celebrate life, to enjoy pastimes, to philosophize, to write poetry, to learn to dance—to be, in a word, human. First, television was going to bring us information faster and in a more enjoyable format than ever before. In the future, we were told, children would know more and be more literate and better educated at an earlier age than any generation preceding them. Fifty years later, that inflated claim needs no further comment. And it would be hard to argue that television has brought us any more or better free time.

Next came computers. In the future, we were told, workers would be freed. Computers were going to enter factories in the form of robots, and offices in the form of the personal computer. They would perform the drudgery, and workers would be liberated to be creative, fully self-actualized human beings. Well, computers and robotics have freed many workers, only it has been called downsizing. Those workers lucky enough to keep their jobs find themselves faced with vastly increased work expectations as a direct result of these "time-saving" devices. If a typist could once produce five pages of text per hour and perhaps thirty or forty pages over the course of a day, that same worker must now produce double or triple that amount to stay competitive.

The computer, the tool that was supposed to liberate the human spirit by saving time (and paper!) has instead become master, piping an apparently endless tarantella to which we all must madly dance. The future has arrived, and the result is a world where, far from having more control of our time, we actually have much less. In our modern world, we allow intrusions into our personal time that would be viewed as tyrannical if they came from a political quarter rather than from the world of work.

Pagers, e-mail, voice mail, the idea that we must be accessible twenty-four hours a day, 365 days a year have all conspired to make us more obsessive-compulsive about time than even Karen Horney could have predicted. Recent advertisements for cell phones show a man keeping contact with the office while sitting in a boat (presumably on vacation), fishing. The ad promises that we will never again have an excuse for not returning a message. The erosion of personal time, not its expansion, has been the result of the introduction of so many so-called time-saving devices. Pagers and cell phone systems sell themselves by advertising larger and larger footprints in which we can be tracked down so that we will not waste time or miss connections. Advertising has convinced us that we must maintain a connection to the hectic world of fleeting time, for if we don't, the feeling goes, the future will leave us in its wake. Time will march on, the future will arrive with us or without us, and the price we must pay to stay in step is to sacrifice our "personal time."

Today, many of us feel deep down that, like Goethe's Faust, we have sold our souls. What we took for knowledge and power really turned out to be confusion and a sense of power- lessness. It is as though we have simply obliterated the time mode we used to call sacred time and have reduced everything to the flat horizontal plane of accelerated linear time. We have traded our "soul time" for a TV dinner and a box filled with microchips. Is there a way to undo this devilish bargain? I be- lieve there is, and in the process we will be able to recover that part of our selves, our very souls, that lives outside the flow of time in what used to be called eternity. A story from the Jewish tradition may show us the way. It is the ancient legend of the golem.

The word *golem* occurs only once in the Bible, in Psalm 139:16, where it has the meaning of "something unformed and imperfect."[8] It is sometimes translated as "embryo." A Talmudic legend refers to Adam as a golem in the first twelve hours of his existence. In Jewish lore, the word was later applied to a legendary creature rabbis created to demon- strate their own metaphysical prowess and the power con- nected with the sacred name of God and the letters used in the Torah generally.

In the earliest forms of the legends, the golem were spirits, but by the seventeenth century they had become physical creatures, usually human in form, that performed tasks for their makers. The most famous version of the legend concerns

Rabbi Loew of Prague. According to this eighteenth-century legend, retold by Isaac Bashevis Singer and alluded to at length by Cynthia Ozick in her novel *The Puttermesser Papers*, Rabbi Loew molded a man-shaped creature out of earth and brought it to life by writing the secret name of God on a piece of paper and slipping it into the creature's mouth. (In other versions of the golem legend, the Hebrew word *emet*, truth, was inscribed on the creature's forehead to bring it to life. Both of these versions, as we shall see, are relevant to our study of time.)

Rabbi Loew originally created the golem to help him complete tasks on the Sabbath, when no devout Jew could work. Since the golem did not possess a human soul, it could perform necessary work during the sacred time of Sabbath, even though it could not make up part of the minyan necessary for temple service. The golem, however, soon caused problems. As the creature grew from day to day, its strength increased, and because it had no soul it used its power blindly, without moral direction. In most versions of the tale, the golem eventually ran amok, destroying property, endangering lives, and, in one version of the story, threatening the synagogue itself.

There was only one way to stop a golem. Its creator had to confront it and somehow get the name of God out of its mouth, or in the case of the golem created by inscribing *emet* (truth) on its forehead, to erase the first letter of the word, leaving only the Hebrew word *met* (death), which effectively killed the creature.

Many modern writers have used the legend of the golem to call attention to the dangerous aspects of technology in the modern world. Bavarian writer Gustav Meirink in his 1915 novel *Der Golem* created a frightening modern allegory about the dehumanizing aspects of modern technological society.

Mary Shelley's *Frankenstein* shows us how the things we create sometimes turn on us and threaten to destroy us if we forget to maintain the proper relationship to them, and a slew of modern science fiction novels and films continue the moral of the tale of the golem with mad scientists and soulless robots run amok. The legend of the golem serves as a perfect metaphor to describe our modern relationship with the clock. Like a golem, the clock is a soulless machine, originally designed to perform work for us. Over time its power grew. We created it to measure time, but today it measures us.

Some years ago, while traveling through rural Japan, I was amazed to see many old women in the countryside who could barely stand up. They walked about hunched over until they almost resembled hoops. It was shocking to see so much physical deformity in a sophisticated first-world country. And then I began to notice the work Japanese country women performed. They swept streets and sidewalks with old-fashioned short-handled brooms. They cut grass with hand croppers that forced them to bend over. They served meals stooped over floor-level tables. Over their lifetimes, the tools they used and the way they did their work deformed their bodies.

In our postindustrial world, the clock is the tool we use most. It is the underpinning of our modern way of life. It makes possible the computers, television programs, and schedules by which we live. The clock measures time in a unidirectional and linear way. This is horizontal time, the time of the workplace and the calendar. Our modern method of time reckoning is perhaps the most pervasive "invisible technology" we live with in the modern world. And for most of us, clock time is the only conception of time that we have. It moves us relentlessly from the past into the future at an ever-faster pace, whether we want to go or not. Like the golem, our mechanical sense of time has come to threaten all we hold dear—our families, our relationships, even the sacred places within ourselves. Living only by clock time, we deny ourselves access to other modes of time, which we could call "soul time," modes that move in very different directions and in very different rhythms from clock time.

Like the short-handled Japanese broom, the accelerated life we are living is shaping us in ways many of us would rather not be shaped. A mind conditioned by the fast rhythms of computers and television is going to operate quite differently from a mind cultured by such slow, patient activities as reading and writing by hand. A day or a lifetime spent interacting with tools that force us to think in nanoseconds or that communicate to us in ten-second sound bites will mold us in ways that slow meditation and contemplation will not. There is mounting evidence we are being deformed by our narrow definition of time.

Recent studies, cited in Jeremy Rifkin's *Time Wars*, show that people who work with computers a great deal are actually beginning to act like computers. Just as a computer multitasks—going from one activity to another, leaving off one function when a bit of information has been communicated and not returning to that site until a new bit is ready—so too people who work with computers all day communicate in short, discrete bits only to those who need information for this or that task. Then off they go to the person who needs the next bit, and so on, returning to the first person only when they have a new bit of information relevant to where they broke off their last conversation. This, of course, is a sort of communication, but it is mere information transmission, which may be the least satisfying form of human communication there is. The human repertoire of communication skills is amazingly sophisticated, capable of bonding people together, of influencing emotions, of expressing complex realities. It is the most powerful socializing tool of our species. But when only data are being communicated, those many levels of human interaction are lost. Pleasantries, social bonding, love, friendship, and affection are becoming less and less a part of normal human intercourse. That kind of communication has been all but replaced by mere information processing as our minds, shaped by our tools, mimic the machines we work with.

But how can we change it? "You can't fight progress," we are told, and that is another of the unquestioned assumptions of our age. Yet we may still be able to get control of the accelerating clock and lessen its impact on our lives. We must do it the same way the rabbi got control of the golem before it destroyed the synagogue. The golem, we must remember, only came to life when the creator inserted the name of God in its mouth, in other words, when the maker invested a lump of clay with divine qualities that it could not bear because it was merely a tool. The word truth on the golem's forehead vivified it, but the word could not give the creature a soul. As the Hebrew pun reveals, the word truth that brought the creature to life is very close to the word death, appropriate for the inert matter out of which the golem is made. Created for the best of purposes, even intended to help us in our observance of sacred time, the golem that we call clock time grows more powerful by the day until it threatens to destroy the very sacred edifice it was meant to serve.

The erosion of private life, including time to oneself, and the erosion of leisure, so important to the experience of sacred time, have resulted from our surrender to the tyranny of *chronos*, or clock time. Because of it, we have lost touch with what used to be called eternity. How, in spite of all, can we free ourselves from this golem and get back to those other dimensions of time, including sacred time, that we experience in the deeper parts of ourselves and that, in recent years, we have increasingly lost contact with?

Fortunately, here and there, like islands, are places where sacred time has not been lost. It is dawn, the sky barely tinged with gray. In a Zen monastery in Kyoto, a monk settles onto a meditation cushion. He arranges himself in the lotus position, his buttocks and knees forming a tripod to support his upper body. He slowly and carefully forms the mudra of meditation, placing his left fingers on top of his right fingers, his thumbs almost touching, as if cradling an invisible egg. Unhurried, he closes his eyes halfway as he faces the wall of the zendo. He focuses only on his breathing, and the air flows smoothly in and out of his lungs. In the incense-filled room, a bell rings softly. Soon his breathing becomes even more regular, almost sleeplike, and he feels the center of his consciousness falling lower, below the relatively fast pace of his conscious thought. He experiences a slowing down. As he remains motionless during the *sesshin*, or sitting period, he feels the edges of his body become less defined: the separation between the inner and the outer world becomes less definite, and a sense of calm and well-being comes over him. His mind hovers in a state between waking and sleeping. Simultaneously alert yet not highly focused on any one thing, he may feel an inner connection with things normally experienced as separate. A bird cries in the distance. Is the bird within or without? The incense in the room comes into his lungs with each breath, and he exhales a bit of himself into the atmosphere as well. His ego seems to dissipate like the smoke. That is all there is. Eventually a bell rings softly. How much time has passed? A few minutes? A half an hour? An eternity? He is not sure. Does it even matter?

In the basilica of Santa Maria Maggiore in Rome, I attended Mass on Palm Sunday a few years ago. The incense rose from the altar through the fifth-century nave, past the Gothic and baroque adornments, toward the ancient coffered ceiling. The congregants clasped palm branches reverently as the choir sang a Gregorian chant. Two thousand years after the beginning of Christianity, the words and gestures of the past were being reenacted. I had the sense that the wall of time has been erased, that the priests concelebrating the Mass were mere vehicles of an ancient mystery. When I emerged from the basilica on to the busy Roman streets, I felt I was leaving behind a permanent reality and entering an ephemeral dream.

Other islands of eternity float in the sea of time. In the U.S. Midwest, the spires of white clapboard churches rise toward the perfectly blue sky. Those needles topped by crosses are often the highest points on the landscape, rising above the fields of corn and wheat. They glow in the summer sun. Through the open windows come the sounds of reedy organs and untrained voices rising in the vibrant strains of Protestant hymns.

Satisfying time hunger is possible. As in the ancient Jewish legend, it involves taking the name of God out of the mouth of the monster, erasing the word truth from its forehead, and relegating clock time again to its status as tool and servant, not master. This will involve rediscovering the many other temporal modes besides clock time in which we human beings can exist.

These are the time modalities in which we experience life as slower, more cohesive, and more energizing than in the clock world where most of us are forced to live. We might think of them as vertical modes. Where horizontal time moves along only toward death, the vertical or sacred time modes, accessible through prayer, meditation, artistic creativity, and many other means, bring with them a sense of refreshment and of being in touch with sources of ongoing life that are somehow outside the vicissitudes of time and death, that are, in a word, eternal.

We have so forgotten how to get to these places where time does not press on us as heavily as it does in our day-to-day lives, that most of us have been approaching the problem of modern life's frenetic pace the wrong way. We have been asking how to manage time, how to save it, how to use it more efficiently, but these approaches diminish our lives and lead only to frustration. There is another way to experience time, one that finds it a friend, not an enemy, that concentrates on its creative possibilities rather than its devouring aspect. It points us to a way to live in which there is world enough and time enough.

In soul time, time can creep or fly or even seem to move backward depending on one's mood, circumstances, or perhaps even hormone levels. Down in the deeper levels of our brain, categories of past, present, and future become fluid, having no distinct boundaries or directions. On some levels of vertical consciousness (dreams, memories, daydreams), time may not exist at all. In this dimension of our being, we somehow feel in contact with eternity. As we'll see later, this vertical dimension of time may be physiologically based. What we call the past may have a phylogenetic component that consists of the biologically stored memories of our (and other) species extending backward in time some hundreds of millions of years. In that sense, we all carry the deep survival instincts of our species, accumulated over millions of years, within us, and we can access these in states of meditation or prayer. We have tended to ignore these older parts of the brain as being too primitive. Modern physiology and neurology, however, are beginning to understand the role of the deep brain, particularly the limbic system, in connection with dreaming and in moving material into the long-term memory where it constitutes our personal "past." Further research on the neurophysiology of ritual trance, conducted by Charles Laughlin and Eugene D'Aquili, shows that there are biological components in the experience of what we call timelessness that involve sophisticated mechanisms of entraining triggered by, among other things, religious rituals.

One of the great gifts of our species is the ability to talk with a measure of detachment about a subject as complex and deeply interwoven in our being as time. Thanks to our higher cognitive abilities, we can separate time processes from ourselves and talk about them objectively, as though time were a thing "out there." Though we can never separate ourselves completely from our experience of it, objectifying time this way, talking about it, understanding it in all its dimensions could lead us back to an ability to experience time in all its fullness once again and not to be so tyrannized by the golem of clock time.

Large numbers of people today feel they are leading what could be called disynchronous lives; that is, they feel that the various parts of their lives are not moving in time with each other. People find themselves torn between the fast-paced rhythm of their outer world and those other, slower rhythms that seem very much a part of human nature but that no one seems to be able to help us connect with. Is it possible to synchronize all the wild and varied rhythms of our being and to achieve once more a state of harmony, calm, and peace that seems so lacking in our modern world? It is, but first we must see more clearly how we got to the strange time and place in which we now find ourselves. Only then will we be able to free ourselves a little bit from the tyranny of the clock and re-discover the slower rhythms of soul time that lie dormant within us. That is the purpose of this book.

Just as in psychotherapy patients need to articulate their problems before they can take effective action against them, so we modern people need to understand just how our clock ob-session and compulsion came to be if we ever hope to return to those slower rhythms of our being that lead to peace and calm. Though the journey may seem long, the destination is never very far away. It lies within us, in the deep core of ourselves where time meets eternity as it does in no other creatures.

CHAPTER 2

A Sense of Timing

NOT LONG AGO, you could tell what time of year it was simply by noticing what foods were in front of you, but one recent January morning, I found myself eating fresh strawberries for breakfast. In my part of the world, strawberries, asparagus, and rhubarb are harvested in the spring, blueberries in midsummer, and corn, tomatoes, and other vegetables in August and September. In late autumn it's pumpkins and squash, then winter root vegetables like turnips. Not that long ago, foods from one season would not have been available in another, unless they were preserved or dried. Today, however, one can have fresh strawberries at virtually any time of the year.

This doesn't amount to much by itself, of course. So we can eat fresh spring fruit in the middle of winter; isn't that an unmitigated boon? Some people happen to enjoy "fresh" out-of-season produce, even though what passes for fresh in winter never has the savor of in-season stuff. (As exhibit A, try one of those wax baseballs that appear in February advertised as "vine-ripened tomatoes.")

Still, eating foods out of season serves as a good example of the problem of the loss of sacred time. We've grown so used to being out of touch with the natural rhythms of life that we may not even notice anymore when we're out of sync.

Seasonal changes, the solstices and equinoxes, which people once celebrated with festivals and holy days, now come and go with little notice. Well, so what? Does it make any difference? I think it does.

Up until the Industrial Revolution, virtually everyone was profoundly affected by seasonal change. The rhythm of work varied with the cycle of nature. People planted in the spring, reaped in the fall. The work they did day to day changed with the growing season. Depending on the weather, they worked in the fields or in the barns, their tasks paralleling the growth of crops. There was celebration at the closure of harvest, and the alternation of seasons was celebrated at festival times that in turn commemorated great mythological events. The winter solstice brought to mind the birth of Jesus or the exploits of solar deities like Rama or Mithras, who overcame the threatening universal dark.

Today, the sense of one's work and life being attuned to larger cosmic rhythms is mostly gone. A stockbroker friend recently complained that he never sees an end to his work. Each day the market opens and closes, rises or falls, but from day to day the work seems the same to him. Winter or summer, the trading of stocks and bonds proceeds, disconnected from anything larger than itself. Quarterly business reports are not tied to nature at all. Neither are fiscal years. Our work levels time, makes it machinelike in its pace.

For many of us in the modern world, the most significant marker of seasonal change is not the glorious bursts of autumn leaves or the blooming of spring flowers but the coming of a new TV season. Even holidays that used to be based on celestial phenomena (Christmas near the winter solstice, Easter near the first full moon after the vernal equinox) have degenerated into mere commercial seasons, with time being measured by so many shopping days before them. We all sense that "the Christmas season" no longer denotes a movement in the heavens so much as a movement in the retail sector. As a result, Christmastide no longer begins with Advent but with the earliest day retailers feel they can stock their shelves with Christmas goods without appearing totally shameless. The first Christmas catalogs now arrive in July. Halloween starts in late August and full Christmastide somewhere in mid-October. Like other festive events, these former holy days have become so commercialized and extended in time that their significance as unique moments marking the year's passage has been sorely diminished.

I believe these examples are symptomatic of a more profound disynchrony in our lives that separates us not only from the cycles of the seasons but even from the deeper parts of our own beings that operate according to temporal rhythms quite different from clock time. Of course, we must occasionally bow to clock time. Horizontal time moves on. It will never again be 11:45 A.M. on October 17, 1996. Clock time moves forward in a steady metronome beat. Like a river, time flows constantly from the past through the present to the future, and in order to enjoy the benefits of living in society, individuals must bend their own private rhythms to those of the group. People who live out of sync with society tend not to thrive, while those who manage to synchronize their lives with the life of the group are generally rewarded with money or prestige. But in traditional societies, social time bears a closer relation to natural time than it does in ours, and so it resonates in many layers of our psyches. The seasons of our personal and collective lives should keep pace with the seasons of the year.

In our culture's setup, however, the time everyone submits to is the time of the clock, which coldly and impersonally ticks off identical minutes, year in and year out. As historian G. J. Whitrow put it, in the modern world, "we are compelled more and more to relate our personal 'now' to the time-scale determined by the clock and calendar."[1] There are some significant drawbacks in sacrificing too much personal time to the clock this way.

For example, we modern folks place a great premium on the sheer amount of time we work. Our language is full of proverbs encouraging us to keep our noses to the grindstone, our shoulders to the wheel. We are told that idle hands are the devil's plaything. As a consequence, workaholics get rewarded by our society even though their behaviors might be destroying them and their families, who rarely see them, much less get to spend "quality time" with them. Those who shortchange their personal time this way are often promoted in our society. They dedicate their time to the firm, to the business, to the job, and in return we give them power, prestige, and more jobs to do. It is a crazy rhythm.

Years ago, pagers were the special privilege of doctors, who might need to be summoned from social activities to tend to patients in emergencies. These people were always on duty; their private time could be invaded at any moment. In return, we gave them great respect, even held them in awe. They were people so valuable to society that they had no such thing as personal time. Today, pagers and cell phones have become required gear for nearly everyone, from UPS truck drivers to the man who comes to clear your drain of backed-up sewage. Kids on the corner carry them, and so do suburban moms cruising the shopping malls and soccer games. It has been an amazing social transformation. We have decided we all must be accessible to anyone at any time.

Once upon a time, only servants and toadies were on call twenty-four hours a day. Only people of extremely low social status had no personal time. One of the great struggles of the labor movements of the past 150 years was the fight for the right to private time, the right to not be owned by the company or the master when not explicitly on "company time." But today we willingly give away our discretionary time. Thanks to pagers, cell phones, portable fax machines, and so on, our personal lives are always accompanied by a background tension: we never know exactly when our private time will be interrupted by the high-pitched summons of our public world, where something is always happening. By making ourselves ever-accessible, we have guaranteed that our private time will continue to shrink. We may even forget what private time is, just as we have forgotten that strawberries don't grow in January.

"Personal time" is just one aspect of the sense of sacred time we have lost in our culture. Personal time has several characteristics that set it off from the clock time by which we normally live. It is fluid, uneven, and of varying intensity. We generally experience it as richer, more textured, and more cohesive than clock time. It is the time we experience when we let our hair down. It is the difference between the commute to work and a walk along a beach. It is the time we invite people to enter when we say, "Be yourself."

Clock time, on the other hand, is segmented into beats of equal duration and roughly equal intensity. Clock time usually feels disconnected, faster paced, less flexible, and only tangentially connected to our moods and feelings. Anyone who has ever had to punch a time clock knows about this kind of time. Even if all meaningful work has been accomplished for the day, you still must hang around until the clock says you may leave. In school, students who may have questions about science must wait until the clock ends the forty-five-minute English period to ask them. We can all add our own examples: fifteen-minute meetings drag out to an hour because an hour was allocated for them; workdays must be exactly eight hours long, regardless of how much or how little work there is to do; or, worse, our workdays never really end because we sleep with our pagers on our nightstands.

Josef Pieper, the German Catholic philosopher, said that work in our time makes "totalitarian claims" on us that we would not stand for from any other source. Even thirty years ago, he could see how we increasingly allow our clock-dominated work to invade our private lives and force us to abide by its rhythms rather than our own.[2] Imagine the outcry, he wrote, if the government demanded that we all wear devices on our belts so at any moment it could intrude on our private time and request us to perform civic duties. Cries of "Communism!" would fill the air. Yet many of us gladly submit to exactly that sort of tyranny when it arises in the form of more work.

The clock, which was originally to have been our servant, has become our master. And a severe taskmaster it is. Since the Industrial Revolution, significant changes in lifestyle occurred as we shifted away from being an agricultural society. The natural rhythms of rising with the sun and doing a "day's work" (longer or shorter, depending on the season) were replaced by the machinelike regularity of a workday measured in a set number of hours. In the early Industrial Revolution, the workday may have been as long as sixteen hours and was ruled strictly by the clock and the factory whistle. Large numbers of displaced agricultural workers submitted to the tyranny of the clock from economic necessity. Records abound of early factory owners working their "hands" to death at their never-stopping machines. Dickens paints a graphic picture of the dehumanizing conditions in newly industrialized England in his *Hard Times*.

Eventually, through liberal reforms and labor actions, workdays in factories and mines were shortened to a humane length of about eight hours. The reformers' motto was "Eight hours for work, eight hours for sleep, and eight hours to do as we please." Thanks to the nineteenth-century Sabbatarian movement, workers also were blessed with a day or two of rest each week.

It is therefore ironic that while most industrial workers today have shorter workweeks than they did 150 years ago, many if not most postindustrial workers are seeing the length of their workweek creep upward in many subtle ways. Through advanced communication technology, the boundary between private time and work time has grown nearly invisible for many workers. Touted as devices that would free us from the workplace, the new information technology was supposed to reduce the work required of us, allow us to have more time with our families, and let us be more human. Magazines in the 1950s and 1960s never stopped touting the future as a time of unlimited leisure. In fact, however, time-saving technology seems only to have drastically reduced the number of hours we have to ourselves. I am amazed at how many students call my office to leave voice mail messages at two A.M. I have long since taken to turning my home phone off at ten P.M. so that I can be unavailable for at least part of my day.

In Dickens's *Great Expectations*, the character Wemmick, a factotum at the law firm of the terrifying attorney Jaggers, has an "at work" self and an "at home" self divided by several miles and a narrow personal moat. Returning home from a hard day at the office where he has been dealing with the murderers and thieves who make up Jaggers's clientele, he can raise a drawbridge, fire off his ceremonial cannon, and be safe for about sixteen hours from the grim realities of the workplace. In other words, he can, for about two-thirds of his daily life, give rein to those parts of himself he must close off at work. In his private time, he reads, he celebrates birthdays, he has tea with his aged parent and the delightful Miss Skiffins. True, Wemmick's mode of life is a bit schizoid, but it is at least better for the poor clerk than if he had to return to his suburban home in Walworth with a pager on his belt and a fax machine, e-mail, and modem waiting for him with messages relayed twenty-four hours a day by the inexhaustible Jaggers. No moat now is wide enough to cut us off from electronic intrusion. Even the off switch doesn't do much good, as e-mail messages simply go into the queue and wait for us to start up our machines again.

The first requirement of accessing sacred time is being able to separate oneself from the demands of profane time. To enter eternity, you must leave time. That has become increasingly hard to do because it involves, first of all, turning off the many devices by which the world of profane time intrudes on us. How exactly did this harried lifestyle come to be? In the past hundred years or so, the world has shrunk in space and time. New methods of transportation, starting with the railroad in the early 1800s, progressively reduced the psychological size of the world. Europe and Asia, once considered far away when the phrase "the other side of the world" meant something, are now regular destinations for international business and leisure travelers.

As the world of space shrank, so did our sense of time. The transatlantic voyage that once took two months by sailing ship and some five days by ocean liner can now be completed in as little as three or four hours via the Concorde. What was once far away is now near in space and time, so near that our ability to traverse space quickly has even led to a new malady: jet lag, that queasy feeling of fatigue and disorientation we get when the body's biological timing systems get out of sync with local time because of the speed with which we've moved across time zones. The body's natural clocks are slower to reset themselves than the clocks we wear on our wrists.

Jet lag, in fact, may be a good metaphor to describe what we as a culture seem to be suffering. We have come so far so fast in recent years that we may often feel the same anxious sense of being out of sorts that we experience when we de-plane in an unfamiliar corner of the earth. Living in the contemporary world can be like being afflicted with a permanent case of jet lag.

With networks of satellites linking television, telephones, and computers, we have shrunk the global village down to the global apartment building, and we have also considerably compressed time. We have radically shortened what we could call our expectation span, the amount of time we can reasonably expect things to take. What used to take days we now want in hours; what used to take hours we want in minutes; everything else we want right now, if not sooner. Up until the early 1800s, information moving from one place to another on the globe could move no faster than a human being on horseback or the speed of a carrier pigeon. Communications theorists like Marshall McLuhan and Neil Postman have written about how slowly information in this preelectronic period moved. It had to cross real space in real time, and the conditions imposed by those facts resulted in communication that, while slow, at least had the virtue of usually being thought through. It was usually linear, logical, and, in a word, composed. With the coming of trains early in the nineteenth century and especially the telegraph in 1835, information got unlinked from real time and space. The telegraph lines crisscrossing the continent could carry information far faster than any human could travel. By afternoon Texas could have word about the quality of the lobster catch in Maine that morning, though, as Thoreau was one of the first to point out, the value of that piece of information, no matter how quickly delivered, was fairly negligible.

The invention of the telephone in 1876 further compressed time and space, and it communicated information in a way the telegraph did not. A telegraph message, like a letter, must at least be thought through and edited, but a telephone message can be spontaneous and scattered. Whereas a letter may be read when the receiver is ready to read it, a telephone call can come at any time of the day or night. From our perspective only a little more than a hundred years later, it is ironic that the first telephone message from Alexander Graham Bell reportedly was "Come here, Watson, I need you." Watson, minding his own business in the next room, was the first person to have his personal time intruded upon by the new technology.

With the coming of radio after 1910, the world entered the era of true mass communication. It was possible for news and entertainment to travel almost instantaneously to large numbers of people over great distances. Space and time were compressed, with some legendary early results. The outbreaks of panic during Orson Welles's infamous *War of the Worlds* broadcast in 1938, and the reassuring voice of Franklin D.

Roosevelt in his fireside chats as well as Winston Churchill's famous BBC broadcasts during the Battle of Britain brought the world, for better or for worse, closer to being a global village operating on a speeded-up timetable of simultaneity.

Then, less than fifty years ago, television further annihilated time as a factor in communication. In 1962, the first transatlantic satellite link was established connecting the east coast of the United States with Britain. Beneath the umbrella of the communications satellite, the whole world could suddenly experience the same image at the same instant. Who in America can forget John F. Kennedy's funeral or the early space shots? But events kept coming at us, each new one pushing out the old. National satellite links soon became international and global. We grew used to new information assaulting us twenty-four hours a day. Something was always happening somewhere, and we could not afford to miss it. CNN, founded in the early 1980s, was created to fill a void we may never have known existed—the need to be informed and up to the minute on breaking news from places we never heard of.

Meanwhile, in the world of work, a similar acceleration was taking place. The personal computer burst on the scene about 1985, and the pace of life picked up even more. "Immediately if not sooner" was no longer a joke, it was a requirement of business. Fax machines and e-mail made conventional mail seem like "snail mail." Overnight delivery systems kept merchandise moving quickly twenty-four hours a day. A sort of hyperconsciousness of time set in. Tracy Kidder's book *The Soul of a New Machine* captured the intensity of the computer companies' competition to shave a few nanoseconds off their machines' performance.[3]

Measuring time in smaller and smaller increments, trying

to keep up with the capacity of our machinery, somewhere in the past few years we've crossed over a boundary of absurdity where seconds seem like eternities. Our computers' imperious instruction "Please wait," in the form of an hourglass icon or a ticking clock, makes us edgy, even though we are rarely kept waiting for more than a few moments.

"Come here, Watson, I need you." That voice of Alexander Graham Bell was but the first instance of technology's god-like quality to disturb our lives, to make us stop whatever we were doing and attend to a machine. In an apocryphal story from the 1950s, President Eisenhower was taken into the large room where the massive Univac computer was housed. The president was asked to direct a question to the machine, and he typed in, "Is there a God?" The machine supposedly ruminated a moment and then printed out, "There is now."

Today, with personal computers in most workplaces and increasing numbers of homes, with instant links via the Internet to all quarters of the globe, we are subject to a constant flow of decontextualized information, a veritable Niagara Falls of stuff that keeps coming at us. Some is good and some is bad; much of it is useless, but we don't have time to sort it out. A perfect example is the cable Weather Channel, which assumes that for some reason we are supposed to be terribly concerned about the weather in Gila Bend, Arizona, even if we don't live there or intend to travel there that day. The daily flow of e-mail seems to consist largely of little gaseous explosions of thought sent hither and yon instantaneously to clutter up our inboxes. Many of these thoughts may not be worth thinking, but by golly they can get there fast. And before you can sort your way through them, they are replaced by more useless information. We feel rushed, pressed to get through all this stuff as quickly as possible. Where valuable time was once measured in moons or suns, it is now parceled out in seconds. There simply is "no time" for personal time, sacred time, or anything else. If we stop to think, to pray, to meditate, or just to stare at the setting sun over the lake, we are lost.

Today, smaller and smaller increments of time can have major effects on our lives. Reaction times must be shorter. Decisions must be made faster. Timing must be precise, to the second or millisecond. It reaches absurdity sometimes. Scientists now must register "leap seconds" as well as leap years. At midnight on December 31, 1995, for example, atomic clocks around the world were stopped for one second to add a leap second to the year so that superprecise time-keepers could be corrected to account for minor irregularities in the earth's rotation. Such are the needs of modern navigation, communications networks, and satellite tracking that a mere one-second error in time every two or three years can have disastrous results. A plane's navigational systems could be off by miles. This hyperfine consciousness of clock time is not restricted to scientists and navigators, of course. We encounter it even in such mainstream occurrences as sporting events.

Today, in every major race, there is a hidden competitor, the clock. In addition to the other athletes on the field, runners today must compete against time. In the ancient Greek Olympic games, the laurel wreath did not always go to the first runner to cross the finish line. A slower runner who ran with more grace and style could take the prize. In the 1996 Olympics, however, not only did sprinter Michael Johnson beat his closest competitor by several meters in the 200-meter dash, he also astonished the world by shaving 0.34 seconds off the world record, which he himself had set just a few weeks before. Commentators could hardly contain themselves about this "massive" shortening of the record, one that would hardly have been recognized in Olympiads up to 1968 when races were clocked in only tenths of a second. Also in the 1996 Olympics, a British sprinter was disqualified because a timing clock attached to the starting blocks and the starter's pistol showed that he had false started. He left the blocks less than 0.01 second before the starting pistol. Who would have noticed?

Our modern need to keep time with more accuracy boggles the imagination and confounds the slower-moving soul time. Atomic clocks can measure accurately to one-trillionth of a second. How short is that? That's the time needed for a light beam traveling at 186,000 miles per second to traverse the thickness of a playing card.[4] In one measurable nanosecond, the time unit by which we measure the speed of our computers, that same beam will travel about six inches. Five hundred nanoseconds occur when you snap your fingers. Somehow we are supposed to comprehend this.

Was the human organism designed to operate at these fine increments for long periods of time? If not, what happens to us when every moment of our waking day is measured out in seconds and microseconds, when our daybooks are no longer for recording what we have done and what happened to us but serve to tell us where to be at every moment? What happens when we turn our lives over completely to clocks and daybooks and try to keep up?

A few years ago, I attended a fascinating lecture given by John Staudenmeier, S.J., a historian of technology from the University of Detroit–Mercy. His talk was on the hundredth anniversary of the lightbulb and the changes wrought by this apparently innocuous piece of technology now found in virtually every home in the modernized world. With the coming of the electric light, he pointed out, the world effectively did away with the night. Most of us now live in light (real or artificial) from the moment we wake up in the morning until we close our eyes at night. Some of the results of this new way of living are obvious. In fact, electricity was seen as a boon wherever it entered. No more smoky, greasy tallow candles or oil lamps with their ever-present danger of fire. People could read or do needlework at night without eyestrain. Sporting events could be held at night. But there were also other, perhaps less desirable effects. Having good-quality light at night made shift work possible. The workday never had to end. This was great news for factory owners, who could keep their machines running longer and thus increase profit, but the biorhythms of shift workers never caught on.

Turning on the lights also brought about more subtle changes. Staudenmeier pointed out that people do different things in the dark than they do in the light. There is no question, for example, that it is easier to be intimate, psychologically as well as physically, in the dark. People say things to one another in dim or no light that they will not say in the bright light of day or electricity. We reveal our inner selves to others in lower light. In addition, quite simply, we slow down. We cannot move as quickly in the dark. The manic pace of day must be broken. In the dark, our imaginations have freer rein and we are more apt to sing, recite or write poetry, or simply daydream than we are in the prosaic light from a bulb. Living in perpetual light, we also cut ourselves off from the diurnal rhythm of sunrise and sunset our species has lived with for millions of years. The gradual coming of dawn and night seem to serve as natural transitions between states of mind. True, in the dark there may be more crime and violence, as people act out their "darker" impulses, but the night can also be a time when we are released from our focus on the work of the day and gain entry into the secret places of ourselves we don't often visit anymore.

Television, of course, cut us off even further from these wellsprings of creativity and soul time. The electric lightbulb brought light into the home but did not change the essential nature of relationships within it. Television programming, however, comes as a hyperactive guest, bringing into our homes a nonstop, frenetic, and fragmentary flow of diversion, information, tragedy, triumph, and violence that draws the attention of family members from each other from waking until sleep and further erodes the time and atmosphere needed for real interpersonal communication. This fast-paced medium, which is a presence for up to twenty hours a day in some homes, provides the constant background noise to all other human interactions.

As a by-product of decisions we have made about how we work and how we live, about how we keep and pass time, we have lost touch with less hectic dimensions of our lives. In the hurry-up pace imposed on us by our machines, we have lost touch with those slower rhythms that take us into the realm of soul time. Soul time lies along the vertical dimension of our being, the dimension where wisdom, spirit, and eternity reside, where love and insight originate. We don't pay much attention to soul time anymore. We're so busy tinkering with our computers that we don't make time for it, even though wisdom and matters of the heart require time. Becoming wise, after all, is infinitely more complex than designing new computer chips or network systems, for wisdom does not come from simply adding a few more megabytes to our memory. It demands its own pace and complete attention, and it is often antithetical to the fast pace at which we normally live.

The same is true of love and of growth in spirituality and in gaining real maturity (as opposed to simply growing older, which anyone can do). Even if you could do it, adding speed to your wisdom modem would not help. Neither can you download another person into your heart. Love takes time, and more megahertz will not speed up the process.

But we don't seem to have time to give to such undertakings anymore. The world moves on apace, and we feel out of control. We are carried along. What's new today will be obsolete tomorrow, and if we stop to wait for wisdom and love we will be left behind. The motto is "Lead, follow, or get out of the way." Philosophers, poets, and seekers of wisdom need not apply

How did we come to this pass? More important, what can we do about it? How can we save time from the heartbreaking and soul-breaking pace at which we are living our lives? Can we overcome this permanent state of jet lag?

I believe we can, but first we must understand better what time, and in particular sacred time, is.

CHAPTER 3

Time and Eternity

WE SUFFER FROM TIME FAMINE. We are looking for more time, but what is time that we think we can get more of it? Or save it? Or slow it down? Or step outside of it? Do we even begin to understand the sea of time we swim in, much less comprehend the eternity we feel lies outside of it? Time is the least tangible of things, yet our everyday speech is laced with aphorisms involving time: time is money, time is of the essence, be on time. The entry for the word in the *Oxford English Dictionary* extends over seven pages, and its meanings are manifold. We march and play music in time. We can be timely or behind the times, and sometimes we are ahead of our time. We take time outs. And in math we multiply things times each other. The word has so many meanings, in fact, one is tempted to say that it doesn't mean anything at all.

Augustine, in his *Confessions*, expressed his frustration eloquently: "For what is time? Who can easily and briefly explain it? Who even in thought can comprehend it, even to the pronouncing of a word concerning it? . . . What, then is time? If no one ask of me, I know; if I wish to explain to him who asks, I know not."[1] And yet, as he knew, time is the central question of human life, for in it (or through it) we find our way to eternity or not at all.

As early as the seventh century B.C.E. on the Milesian coast of Asia Minor, the pre-Socratic Greek philosophers were preoccupied with the paradox of time. They, like us, experienced the world as a place of unceasing change where each moment flowed into an irretrievable past. And yet, also like us, they had a deep intuition that in some ways nothing changed. On some level of their being, they experienced permanence, even eternity. All of us feel this way.

Put down this book for a moment and carefully examine your hand, back and front. It is the same hand you had as a child, yet everything about it is different. It is larger, perhaps hairier or more gnarled. It may soon start to show age spots or wrinkles. Over the years, millions of cells in your hand have been sloughed off and replaced by new cells until it is no longer even the same flesh that was there decades ago, and yet you feel, deeply and intuitively, that this older hand is the very same hand that laboriously learned to wield a pencil back in first grade.

Everything changes and yet also remains the same. This strange paradox drives our search for sacred time.

Anaximander (c. 610–545 B.C.E.) was the first in the West to name that which lay beneath the ever-changing surface of things. He called it the *apeiron*, or the limitless. Everything in the world of time has limits, but the *apeiron* is forever.

In the fifth century B.C.E. in Ephesus, Heraclitus told us what we all knew: the world of time is like a river; though it looks continuous and eternal, it is really in constant flux. You cannot step into the same river twice, he said, and nothing about life remains the same from one instant to the next. And yet, in spite of that, we are convinced that the ever-changing river is the same from day to day. Why do we feel this?

Heraclitus concluded that some underlying principle must

run through rivers and people keeping them the same in spite of constant change, and he called it the *logos*. This Greek word literally meant "word," but it also carried connotations of rational intelligence, as do its English descendants logic and logical" *Logos*, a rational, timeless intelligence, was built into the nature of the world. *Logos* was also a quality of the human mind, and as a result human beings possess the unique ability to see through the ever-shifting surface of things and to experience the unity, order, and permanence that exists beneath the flux.

Zeno and Parmenides, in the fifth century B.C.E., tried to articulate the exact relationship between the changing world of time and the permanent world of eternity by focusing on our experience of change. Parmenides pointed out an obvious problem: if things in this world are constantly in the process of changing, they never really *are*. At every moment, every thing is becoming something else. As soon as you think you have put your finger on what a thing is, it has already changed from what it was when you first laid eyes on it. And if the entire world is constantly changing, then can we say that it exists at all?

Zeno (c. 490–430 B.C.E.) tried to talk about the moment we call the now. It is constantly in motion, he said, like an arrow in flight. An arrow's flight, Zeno said, can be thought of as a succession of still moments, one arrow's length replacing another as it moves through its arc. Similarly, he said, time can be thought of as a succession of moments we call "now," where one "now" replaces another the way one arrow's length replaces the previous one. But there is a problem with the analogy. Unlike an arrow, a "now" is not a physical object. It doesn't occupy space. The moment we call the now is infinitely divisible. Zeno used the hypothetical example of a frog that jumped halfway toward a pond forever and never fell in, though it came infinitesimally close. No matter how quickly we say the word *now*, no matter how finely we divide time, the moment we intended to name slips away into the past before we can name it. How, therefore, can we say that now exists?

Modernity may have exacerbated our sense of time's slipping away, or may have led us to feel it is moving faster now than in the past, but the sense of time's impermanence has been with us for a long time. Zeno put his finger right on the paradox of time and eternity.

Real things, said Parmenides and Zeno, have to possess certain qualities. They must have unity, indivisibility, indestructibility, and unchangeability. But in the physical world we experience only fragmentation, destruction, and constant change in all things. And yet, in spite of that, we also sense from time to time something that is permanent and continuous. Where does this sense of permanence come from? Is it in the world or in ourselves?

The Pythagoreans, a sect of philosophers who flourished 525–350 B.C.E., said that the answer lay in mathematical and musical combinations. The unseen and unchanging One manifests itself in various forms, they said, but, like the vibrating string of a lyre, the One cannot be seen. However, we can see its effects, just as we can hear the invisible string of the lyre. Unchanging mathematical relationships, like the famous Pythagorean theorem, express eternal realities. The equation $a^2 + b^2 = c^2$ was true always and everywhere. The Pythagoreans had found something that seemed to exist outside the world of time: pure ideas. The human mind could give us access to the unchanging, permanent, timeless reality that lay beneath the world of time. Ideas, from the Greek word idein, to see, were the link between the world of time and the realm of timelessness. They allowed us to see into eternity.

This notion was taken further by Plato. He said that a world of Forms existed outside the physical realm of change and time. One gained access to this timeless world through the rational intellect. In his famous allegory of the cave, he described our situation as like that of slaves seated in a cave facing a blank wall. A source of great light comes from behind us, yet we don't turn toward it. Between the light and our backs, objects pass back and forth and cast their shadows on the wall in front of us. These moving shadows are what we normally take for reality in the world of time. But occasionally someone, a philosopher, say, will turn and see the actual forms that are casting the shadows and thus gain a better apprehension of the truth, and those who gaze past even the Forms will see the ultimate source of light itself, the sun, endlessly burning, unitary and bright in the timeless realm. The source of light is eternal, and we "see" it with our minds.

But what exactly was the relationship between the world of time in which we existed and the timeless realm in which the Forms existed? Granted we humans might be able to see into both worlds, we still must ask how the two realms were put together. Here was the rub. Time and eternity were related to each other, but how? We have difficulty even finding the right prepositions to talk about it. We say eternity is above, or beneath, or behind, or below the world of time. We say we can reach through time and touch eternity. Yet none of these expressions entirely satisfies. Plato addressed these questions at some length in his dialogues, without much success. In *The Statesman* and *Parmenides*, he provides summaries of myths about time and of the pre-Socratic philosophers' ideas but never convincingly brings together time and eternity.

Aristotle thought these questions were worth enough thought that he devoted books III and IV of his *Physics* to analyzing them. He paid less attention to eternity than the other philosophers did and instead focused on the world of time. He said that time and change are bound together inextricably. Time is the stick by which we measure change, and change is the way we recognize time's passing. The largest possible sphere of change, according to Aristotle, is the motion of the heavens. All other, smaller changes, and thus time itself, are measured by that largest of all movements. Ultimately, he concluded, time must be circular, like the apparent motion of the planets around the earth. Time, for him, was a great cycle of Eternal Return. But, with all due regard to the Philosopher, if time is the measure of change and change reveals time's passage, we are left with little more than a tautology.

As the classical age wound down, the ideas of Plato and Aristotle were further articulated, but no one really got beyond the essential paradox of the apparent coexistence of time and eternity. The neo-Platonic philosophers further developed the contrast between time and eternity but could not bring the two together. Time (the realm of past, present, and future) involved change. Eternity, on the other hand, was an ever-changeless now to which all times were equally present.

Plotinus (205–270? C.E.) said that the eternal realm, which he called *aion,* was all encompassing and contained all contradictions, including apparent distinctions between past, present, and future. In *aion* there was neither earlier nor later (*proteron, husteron*). You can only say it "is," and when you had said that, you were finally talking about eternity. *Aion,* for Plotinus, was a whole without parts. It was everything all together as if in a single point, yet it was not of any size. It was also, of course, outside of time (*achronos*).

If this sounds familiar to those of us raised in the Christian tradition, it's because Christianity incorporated these very distinctions through Origen and Boethius and used this language to talk about God and his eternity.

But the neo-Platonists still left the problem of articulating just how time and eternity are related. Tatian (120–173 C.E.) said we are like passengers on a ship who can sometimes get the mistaken notion that the shore is floating away when it is really the ship and its passengers that are moving. So, too, *aion* (eternity) stands still and unmoving while temporality flows on. We are fooled by time's illusion. This idea later influenced Augustine, who identified eternity with God and temporality with the world of humankind.

Augustine was also influenced by another idea, first proposed by Alexander of Aphrodisias (fl. c. 205 C.E.), who suggested that time may exist primarily in the mind. The flow of time is a unity, but our minds divide it into the multiplicity we call past, present, and future. Augustine expanded on this and identified past, present, and future with three mental states: memory, attention, and expectation.[2]

The problem never seems to be resolved in philosophy. In the Western world, our sense of time has remained somewhat fragmented, the dual nature of our experience of time and eternity never satisfactorily articulated. Perhaps the question of time is just too complex for rational philosophy, which has a tendency to divide things into either/or categories. The Greek philosophers did well when describing either time or eternity, but talking about the relationship between them seemed more difficult. When the Greeks talked about time in their mythology, however, they seemed to get at some truths that they couldn't broach in their philosophy. And perhaps we too can use mythology to better understand time's paradoxical nature and thus come to a clearer understanding of sacred time.

In Hesiod's *Theogony*, we discover the origin of time's apparent ability to devour and destroy everything in this world, and, because it is a myth, the tale also shows the way to immortality. In the beginning, there was only the Void. Then Gaia, the Earth, appeared. After Gaia came Eros (Desire), which brought forth the sky god, Ouranos, who had sex with the Earth and impregnated her. Gaia gave birth to three horrid monsters with one hundred heads and fifty hands each, and Ouranos forced them into the earth against Gaia's wishes. Later, Gaia and Ouranos produced other children, but Gaia remained angry at Ouranos for having hidden her first offspring away. She called on her other children to wreak vengeance, and her son Kronos was brave enough to accept the challenge. Kronos castrated his father with a flint sickle while the old man was trying to make love to Gaia. The wounded Ouranos cursed Kronos and prophesied that he would one day be overthrown by his own son. Kronos then married his sister Rhea, and together they produced many children.

Almost all of the early children of Kronos and Rhea were personifications of the negative aspects of the world of time: Doom, Fate, Death, Dream-troubled Sleep, Blame, Grief, the three Fates, Nemesis, Deception, Old Age, and Discord. Out of Eris, the goddess of discord, came Kronos's grandchildren: Toil, Forgetfulness, Famine, Pain, Battles, Fights, Murders, Manslaughter, Lawlessness, Recklessness, and False Oaths. Hesiod includes a two-hundred-line catalog of names of additional creatures and monsters born of the Titans.

Eventually, Kronos forced himself on Rhea and fathered the Olympian gods and goddesses. However, Kronos, remembering the curse of Ouranos that he himself would be overthrown one day by one of his children, swallowed them the moment they were born.

As his scythe indicates, Kronos was originally an agricultural god. In earlier versions of the Greek myth of creation, he presided over a golden age, but by the fifth century B.C.E. he had become identified with time (*chronos*) and its destructive aspects. Kronos's scythe and his cannibalistic appetites became emblems of time's destruction, which knows no limits. *Chronos* is the name for the kind of time whose quick passing we fear so much. From moment to moment, time eats us, and we know that our lives will not last forever. The myth tells us that time, the hungry father god, will eventually swallow us all into the darkness of death. The myth is so persistent that Kronos's scythe is still carried by the New Year's caricature of Father Time and by the personification of death known as the Grim Reaper, who also bears an hourglass nearly run out. In world mythology, time and death often go hand in hand. In Hindu tales, Kala, Time, is associated strongly with Yama, the god of death. The message should be clear from Hesiod's catalog of the early offspring of this god: the world dominated by Chronos, as we should spell his name when he represents time, is the monstrous world of pain, suffering, and death. Is there no escape?

Fortunately, the myth tells us, time, death, and destruction do not triumph. Time has a dual aspect. Kronos, the child eater, was originally an agricultural god and, as Plato noted in *Timaeus*, he once presided over an age of fertility and growth. He was first a fertile spirit, capable of bringing life into the world, even if he didn't always nurture it. He begets his children before he eats them. Time is first a life giver, then a life taker.

Frustrated and angry at seeing her children destroyed by their father, Rhea escaped to Crete and gave birth to her youngest son, Zeus. She hid him in a cave on Mount Aigaion, where he was suckled by his grandmother Gaia, Earth herself. To trick Kronos, Rhea wrapped a stone in swaddling clothes and fed it to the ever-hungry father god, telling him it was Zeus. When Zeus reached maturity, he and Rhea made Kronos vomit up the other children, and Zeus led the regurgitated Olympians in a horrific battle against Kronos and the other Titans, finally toppling them into Tartarus, where they remained concealed in a misty gloom surrounded on all sides by bronze walls. By this victory, Zeus and the other Olympian deities came to immortality.

These myths show us how the Greeks understood the dual nature of time. In fact, they actually had separate words for the life-taking and the life-giving aspects of time. The first, *chronos*, meant time in its more destructive manifestations, but the other word, *kairos*, meant moments when time presented us with possibilities of action, decision, and, most of all, opportunity. In fact, *kairos* was personified as the god Opportunity, a man with wings on his shoulders and heels, scales balanced on a knife edge, carrying the wheel of Fortune and sporting a forelock by which he could be grabbed and mastered. To "grab time by the forelock" meant to seize the opportunity presented by the moment. In *kairos*, time's cannibalistic quality was subordinated to its ability to bring forth possibilities. In Iranian-Mithraic mythology, this idea of time was personified in the figure known as Aion, a lion-headed god wrapped in a serpent. This god, according to G. J. Whitrow, represents eternity, and the snake wrapped around him like a mummy's bandages represents time. The snake's body is sometimes decorated with zodiacal symbols, representing the path of the sun and stars, and connects the figure with the Iranian god of time, Zurvan. This strange figure, about which Carl Jung commented at length in *Aion: Researches into the Phenomenology of the Self*, symbolized the eternal and inexhaustible creativity of time, for just as time devours us from minute to minute, so too from minute to minute it brings everything in the world into existence and sustains the whole universe as long as we and it exist. Time the destroyer is the more obvious manifestation in our world, but time is also the medium in which creativity occurs, and as long as things exist time sustains them. It is through the things brought forth by time that we may partake of the world of eternity.

The message found in mythology is clear: the world of pain and death, dominated by the destructive aspect of Time, is not the be-all and end-all. Just as Zeus and the other gods achieved immortality, so may we. Other mythological traditions tell us the same thing. Jesus was swallowed by the earth and was disgorged again three days later, and Rama died and rose again to conquer the demon Ravana in the Hindu *Ramayana*. These gods serve as models for us so that even we modern time-bound creatures may find a way to become immortal. To do that, however, involves a new or, perhaps more correctly, a very old way of looking at time. But what is that way? How do we reach out to eternity? How do we pierce the veil of time and bring eternity into the here and now? How do we find our way to that place the Greeks called *apeiron* or *aion*, whose aspects seem to be beyond limits and change, the source of all that comes to be?

The answer lies, I think, in the various religious traditions of the world, with their myriad ways of ritual, prayer, and meditation. Perhaps these give us a method to resolve the paradox of time and eternity. For the Greeks, rites like the Eleusinian mysteries and the religious ecstasies of Dionysian worship allowed them to exist in a third realm, the realm of ritual time, which belonged neither to the world of time nor to the world of eternity but in a threshold space between them that we can call sacred time.

Perhaps the best way to approach a definition of sacred time is to talk about various temporal rhythms we experience. We become attuned to rhythms almost from the moment we are conceived. Our lives have their origins in the rhythmic movements of sexual intercourse. Our mother's heartbeat, which we hear after the auditory nerve develops in the sixth month of pregnancy, is an introduction to the beat of the world.[3] Her regular movements and times of sleep, the sounds of the world filtering through the womb all suggest that there is a regular pulse to our existence in the world. Our birth is signaled by a change in rhythm as the contractions of our mother's uterus expel us into the world. Babies are bounced rhythmically on their parents' knees, they are sung to, they learn language by chanting nursery rhymes. As we grow, we learn other rhythms: day and night, sleep and waking, hunger and satisfaction. Eventually, we learn to dance in time to the rhythms of our tribe. (The present-day Odawa in Michigan allow their children to fall asleep around the ceremonial drum so that they absorb the pulse of their people even in their dreams.)

Rather than experiencing time as the steady beat of a clock and eternity as a complete stillness, we actually experience a number of different times, expressed as various beats or tempos. Internally, our bodies are a complex hierarchy of rhythms. Heartbeat and respiration are only two of the more obvious cadences. When we sleep, the rhythm of our breathing slows down. When we run or exercise, it speeds up. When we feel fear or passion, our heart rate increases; when we meditate, it slows. Ingestion and excretion, waking and sleeping are rhythms of which we are more or less conscious. Others, like the secretion of hormones, operate on rhythms of which we are unaware. These rhythms are carefully synchronized with each other by physiological systems, and when they are operating correctly we feel "in sync."

In addition to physical rhythms, we also live in a milieu of cultural rhythms, such that crossing cultures involves learning new and different tempos as well as learning new languages. On a recent trip to Italy, some Dutch friends were appalled that their train did not depart Florence at the exact moment it was scheduled to leave. The Italians on board seemed not to mind or even notice much. In the Netherlands, apparently, it is a matter of national honor that the trains leave the station exactly when the second hand reaches twelve at the appropriate minute. Similarly, the leisurely Mediterranean lunches of southern France and Spain seem slow to Americans, with our notion of eating as a function to be completed as quickly and efficiently as possible. In Parisian café society, a cup of coffee may take a half hour to arrive, but no one seems to mind. In the United States, we want it hot and now. To many a northern European or American, the idea of closing down an entire city for three hours while people eat lunch or take a siesta seems an appalling waste of time.

Needless to say, the idea of being on time varies greatly from culture to culture as well. In Germany, one must be *pünktlich* to the moment, while in Tokyo "on time" means arriving a little bit early. In rural Ireland, however, time moves differently. Some Norwegian Minnesota friends of mine were taken aback when they arrived "on time" for a dinner invitation only to find that their Irish hosts were not even home. Arriving several hours later, the hosts were surprised that my friends had taken them at their word timewise. I myself remember the nonchalance with which a Kuwaiti student arrived at my office on a Thursday afternoon for a Tuesday morning appointment. For him, it was only important that he was there. For me, it was important that he was there at the wrong time. The difficulty we had settling the matter was due only in part to the language barrier between us. We were in quite different temporal universes.

One thing, at least, should be clear from all this. Our time sense thoroughly pervades our experience of what it means to be human. Time is the environment in which we move. We are immersed in it as fish are immersed in the sea, and we experience it as "currents and countercurrents, fed by rivers from different lands."[4] Like the ocean surrounding the fish, time is all around us and flows through us as well. We experience it as vast, varied, impersonal, and outside of us, but we also experience it as something deeply internal. Time forms the invisible background against which we measure nearly all our experiences of daily life. The regular temporal structures of social life—our schedules, in other words—establish the context in which we decide whether events and occurrences are "normal" or not.

The varied, almost limitless rhythms of life and the stillness of eternity—how do we bring them together? The answer may have as much to do with dancing and singing as it does with philosophy. Studies conducted in the 1960s and 1970s confirmed what scientists had suspected for over a hundred years: that the human body, like other organisms, has a circadian rhythm.[5] The human sleep-wake cycle, the oscillation of the body's temperature, and periods of physical activity regularize themselves around a "day" of twenty-four to twenty-six hours, even when subjects are isolated for prolonged periods from such time cues as regular alternation of light and dark or regular mealtimes. (In the most extreme example, French researcher Michel Siffre lived in a total isolation in a cave for two months, and his body kept itself on a rhythm close to twenty-four hours.) In other words, the human body, like other animals' bodies, contains an inner clock whose business is to keep time for the organism. Our intuitive sense that time suffuses our entire existence has a physiological basis.

Through the 1980s, much research was conducted to discover exactly where the neurophysiological clock was located, and researchers now believe there is no single time regulator. Rather, there are at least two major timekeeping systems in the body, one located in an area of the hypothalamus known as the suprachiasmatic and preoptic area, and the other in the pituitary and pineal gland areas of the brain stem. They seem to work together, presumably through neural or hormonal connections, to maintain the stability and regularity of the body's systems. Working in conjunction with external time cues like changes from light to dark or temperature changes, and such social cues as "work time" and "bedtime," the body's inner sense of time stays coordinated with the time and timing of the outer world. When all of our systems are working in harmony with one another and the outer world, we are "in sync."

However, it is possible to desynchronize the body's systems by manipulating the environmental time cues that normally budge the circadian rhythms of the body backward or forward. It is possible, in other words, for the finely tuned time sense most of us carry within us to get scrambled. We can get off the beat and lose the rhythm of life that we usually take for granted.

The most extreme experience of this results from jet lag; a milder version occurs with the twice-yearly time shift of daylight saving time. During these periods, our body's circadian rhythms get out of sync with such environmental cues as sunrise or sunset and with such social cues as mealtimes. It may be nine A.M. in Paris, but my body's clock is telling me it's only three A.M. back home, and I should be asleep. Similarly, my stomach rumbles an hour before or after "lunchtime" for a few days after a time shift. Mealtimes, work times, and sleep times usually readjust to the clock within a few days. Some physiological systems, like body temperature fluctuations and the excretion of various chemical compounds, can take longer to resynchronize, but generally within a week or so everything is back together.

Scientists have discovered that the body resynchronizes faster when people expose themselves to more environmental and social time cues. Experienced travelers know, and research backs them up, that they will adjust to their new time zone more quickly if they go out into the daylight and see people eating breakfast or lunch than if they stay in their hotel rooms with the blinds drawn. That is, it is possible for us to manipulate our time sense and to resynchronize the various rhythms inside and outside us so as to foster a sense of balance and equilibrium.

Perhaps such a mechanism exists in the plethora of religious rituals, prayer methods, and meditation practices that human beings have developed over the millennia. Traditionally, these result in a feeling of harmony between the world of time and the world of eternity and serve to bring individuals and communities into synchrony.

Whether it's the throb of a shaman's drum, the smooth melisma of Gregorian chant, the monotone syllables of Buddhism's *Prajñaparamita-sutra*, the call of the muezzin from the minaret of the mosque, or the beat of the *santeria* drum, nothing so perfectly characterizes a religion as the unique rhythms of its liturgies. In our rituals, we believe we have found the beat of the universe, the pulse of God. People everywhere seem to relate to their gods as if they are putting themselves in sync with a master percussionist.

Sufi dancers whirl themselves into ecstasy, while in Zen temples monks rise slowly from their mats to perform *kinhin*, painstakingly placing the heel of one foot before the toes of the other as they pace the perimeter of the hall like snails. Native Americans circle the sacred drum to a musically simple but socially complex beat. Chanting *om*, the yogi attempts to extend a single syllable as long as breath will permit, while in Protestant churches, souls are stirred by the triumphant pulse of Old One Hundred.

From the outside, we watch each other's religious rites as if they were mere theatrical spectacles. (I remember first seeing Sufi dancers, billed as "whirling dervishes" on *The Ed Sullivan Show*.) But we feel our own rites connect us at the most profound levels of our being with the beat of the universe itself.

The antiphonal give and take of the black gospel choir may seem at odds with the sustained monosyllables of the Orient. Underneath, however, there is a deep commonality, a drive to express the rhythms of our lives in song, dance, and sound, to move our bodies in sync with other bodies, to bring into accord the disparate rhythms within us, and, in the end, to dance with God.

What I am going to suggest next may be surprising, for the point I would like to pursue is that what we call sacred time may involve physiological and cultural dimensions as well as spiritual ones. Perhaps we human beings have a profound physical need for religious ritual and keeping the Sabbath, a need as deep as our need for food, water, and sleep. Perhaps religious rituals, which allow us to cross the threshold between time and eternity, are vital survival mechanisms developed by our species to keep balance in ourselves and in our societies. And perhaps when we try to live a purely secular life we cut ourselves and our society off from a powerful source of balance, well-being, and integration.

Research conducted over the past twenty years by Eugene D'Aquili, Charles Laughlin, and others seems to show that religious devotees' anecdotal reports of feelings of inner peace and harmony are reflections of biological, even neurological changes that follow the practice of such religious disciplines as chant, meditation, and ritual dance. D'Aquili and Laughlin, researchers at the medical schools of the University of Pennsylvania and the University of Ottawa, have amassed a considerable body of research on the physiological and psychological changes wrought by spiritual practice.

According to D'Aquili and Laughlin's research, the rhythmic chanting, dancing, and music that accompany or make up rituals constitute driving mechanisms that entrain, or coordinate, various neural systems in the body. In their view, there is a hierarchy of states of consciousness leading up to a state of exaltation they call "absolute unitary being" (AUB). The least intense level of elevated consciousness is the sort of aesthetic perception and appreciation one experiences when viewing a sunset, looking at a beautiful painting, or listening to certain kinds of music. One may feel a sense of being taken out of oneself and one's normal consciousness of the world. In the case of aesthetic rapture, the focus of attention is the work itself or the natural phenomenon, like a sunset, that inspires it. One loses track of oneself, as it were, and gets absorbed into the object one is admiring. The next state is religious awe, which includes the sort of elevation one feels in the aesthetic state, but added to it is a deep perception of meaning and wholeness in the world, which is both outside and inside of us. Beyond that lies religious exaltation, or cosmic consciousness, in which one senses that the universe itself is essentially unified, purposeful, and good. At the farthest end of the spectrum of expanded consciousness is AUB, a state described by D'Aquili as "nothing but a timeless and perfect sense of meaning and wholeness without any perception of discrete entities."[6] In the hands of poet-mystics like Meister Eckhart, Hildegard von Bingen, or Teresa of Avila, we find descriptions of the self become like a feather on the breath of God, or images of sexual ravishment by a higher power in which the individual human soul is lost in a quasi-orgasmic ecstasy. In this rare mystical state, one experiences absolutely no distinction between oneself, the external world, and the source of all cosmic energy. Everything inside and outside the self is experienced as one.

An essential part of the experience all along the spectrum from aesthetic rapture to mystical vision is that the percipient loses all sense of clock time and feels, for a moment anyway, lifted from the normal flow of history into a timeless realm of art or eternity. Psychologist Mihaly Csikszentmihalyi called this, in his book of the same title, "flow." In the flow state, the individual subject acts spontaneously, apparently without conscious effort, and feels guided by a timeless or eternal intelligence that is simultaneously part of one's self and exterior to it. This is sacred time at its most profound.

The research of D'Aquili and Laughlin locates this experience in processes of the limbic system, including the hypothalamus, hippocampus, and amygdala, in association with the prefrontal cortex, which may act as a synthesizer responsible for the powerful sense of unity that the mystic feels. Religious states less intense than AUB may involve "mild to moderate stimulation of certain neurocircuits of the lateral hypothalamus," which give a more moderate feeling of fear and exaltation, the experience of the fascinating and tremendous mystery that gives rise to the religious impulse.[7]

Given the sense of timelessness effected by religious ritual and meditation states, it should come as little surprise that the neurological structures involved should be many of the same ones as those involved in our time sense. Here we are entering what Jean Guitton, in *Man in Time*, called "the ambiguous zones of consciousness where the biological and the spiritual are sutured."[8] Talking of religious experience as if it were neurophysiology is an attempt to link the biological and the spiritual, but we should not reduce spirituality to mere neurophysiology because, as I discuss below, it extends beyond a mere entraining mechanism for the organism and into a remarkable means for tying together individuals in a society and ultimately for providing a healthy worldview that is prophylactic, in the sense that it helps one to ward off the disillusionment and despair that seem endemic in the modern world. To use physiology to discuss spirituality is to enter an intermediate zone between science and spirituality. We change lenses for a moment to look at something in a new way. Like quantum physicists who regard light as a particle or a wave depending on what they need it to be for a particular discussion, we can talk about biology or spirit when discussing religious experience with the idea that it is really both and neither.

The research of scientists like D'Aquili and Laughlin merely seems to verify what practitioners of religious traditions find obvious: the dramaturgy of religious liturgy, its powerful symbolism, and its methods seem particularly well adapted to foster a sense of unity and timelessness in us. As Laughlin points out, rituals focus our attention on symbols, actions, and objects that a culture has collectively decided are important. Because these symbols (the cross, the host, the Torah, the mihrab that faces Mecca, a simple candle flame) seem given by society or the gods rather than having been created by one individual, they transcend the individual and are invested with emotional power. People respond strongly and on prerational levels to these symbols, and rituals are structured in such a way that they keep the sensorium—the body's total sensory intake—focused on the object or rite, which is to say on the timeless, impersonal realities they represent. Thus, incense, sound, special gestures, and ritual foods take each of the senses in turn and direct our focus toward a sense of greater unity. The sensuous nature of rituals mirrors two complementary processes of the autonomic nervous system, the ergotropic and trophotropic systems, which govern, respectively, states of excitation and of relaxation. Some rituals (chanting, drumming, dance) hyperexcite the ergotropic system; others (Zen-style sitting) stimulate the trophotropic system. The ergotropic system prepares the body to meet situations in the external environment, while the trophotropic system channels the body's energy to processes of "repair, growth and development."[9] Perhaps the growing popularity among Westerners of "quieting" styles of oriental practice is a response to the busyness of modern life, which calls constantly on the ergotropic system so that we live in a more or less constant state of excitation and rarely experience "vegetation, repair, growth and development" of the trophotropic system. As the Psalmist puts it, more poetically, we must "Be still and know I am your God."

In this, we are coming very close to understanding the experience of sacred time. The very names we use for the experience indicate the unifying effect of entering sacred time. Religion, etymologically, means to rejoin things previously separated. Religious practice "re-ligaments" things, as it were. Yoga comes from the same Indo-European root as the English word yoke, indicating the sense that body and soul come together in the various asanas of hatha yoga or the other yogic disciplines.

Sacred symbols and ritual processes, according to Laughlin, actually facilitate the incorporation of new neurological pathways, organizing them in a more complex yet more unified way. The mechanisms of ritual (music, dance, psychotropic drugs, fasting, privation) actually seem to "retune" the autonomic nervous system activities of the participants.[10] Thus sacred symbols, worship, and ritual can, by their penetrating power, dissolve old ways and boundaries of thinking and allow us to reunify ourselves at a higher level of consciousness, more neurologically complex and better integrated. Subjectively, this is reported as an experience of "flow," a loss of ego-self, diminishment of the normal subject-object distinction, a reduction of anxiety, and a gain in clarity, global consciousness, and sense of wholeness. This is the state of consciousness we enter when we enter sacred time.

Subjective reports of how it feels to be in sync describe in detail the conjunction of feelings and emotions that occurs as we approach AUB, or peak moments of spiritual experience. In aesthetic or religious rapture we may feel, as Emily Dickinson did, the hair rising on the head, a combination of attention and relaxation, laughter mixed with tears, an energizing tumult of thoughts and feelings that is difficult to put into words because it transcends human language. There is a slowing down of time, and yet also a speeding up, so that when one is in the flow one is not sure if an hour has passed or a day. In addition, one realizes, with laughter and tears, that this life we live, with all its problems and shortcomings and tragedies, is nonetheless worth living. The Romantic poets called it Joy; others have named it ecstasy, a state in which one feels literally outside oneself and yet is more oneself than ever.

The liminal, or threshold, state of consciousness induced by ritual experience allows us to enter an intermediate zone between normal consciousness and ritual trance. This threshold state is a region where transformations may occur. The psychological study of ritual states shows that rituals offer us a unique way to cross thresholds of human consciousness. By providing a time out of time, a gateway to eternity, the ritual moment permits us to incorporate the past and to open ourselves to the integration of the present and the future. A religious rite of passage is effective because it is a finely evolved mechanism for helping us bridge a gap in the development of our consciousness. The ritual structure carries us over the intermediate zone, or warp, between two phases of psychological development. One enters the *bar mitzvah* a boy and leaves it a man. One comes into the wedding a single person and leaves as part of a married couple. Laughlin goes so far as to say that effective rites actually change neural pathways. "[R]itual manipulation of phase attributes, particularly by means of symbols, may be used to transform the operating neural structures mediating phases of consciousness."[11] In effect, a ritual helps structure an unconscious process, making it more conscious. One might even say that rituals facilitate human development. The rite provides a time-tested way of expanding one's consciousness by providing a doorway or threshold through which we may pass from one level of consciousness to another.

Hall noted the importance of such threshold states. "One is compelled to assume that these different states are functionally advantageous in humans and may be one of the most important feedback mechanisms that tell people how they are doing."[12]

On a psychological level, religion seems to offer us the possibility of developmental transformations in which we achieve a more complex awareness of ourselves as well as the world around us and our place in it. This may be noted subjectively in the sense of being "born again" that many converted people feel, and it may even show up in the way people integrate their own experiences and consciousnesses in new and more complex ways. Presumably the physiology is the same whether one is Sufi dancing or awakening the kundalini in yoga. As a binding element, the religious rite has no equal.

Religious rites and symbols, with their unique ability to penetrate and unify layers of consciousness, provide a powerful way to mark and to effect life changes and to coordinate them with events in the outer world. Because ritual allows us to enter a liminal time, similar to the time of the unconscious, we may dissolve and reconstitute ourselves in the ritual moment. During moments of liminal (or sacred) time, parts come to stand for the whole; elements of the self are changeable and exchangeable during these periods.

In traditional societies, religious rites accompany us on our life journey and become markers of growth. As we pass through the stages of our life journey, these rites serve as mileposts. By baptism or other rites of incorporation, we are brought into the group. In many societies a line is drawn between childhood and adulthood by rites of initiation that come at the time of puberty: in Catholicism, confirmation; in Judaism, *bar* or *bat mitzvah*. In the Mexican culture, the celebrations surrounding a young girl's fifteenth birthday turn the girl, who is already a woman physically, into a psychological woman. Her self-definition changes. The rite of marriage marks a commitment between a man and a woman but also forges the union through its powerful symbolism of uniting two separate beings into one. Rites to mark ordination, death, even (in some traditions) divorce thus signify and seal stages of growth and change throughout our lives.

As the clock ticks away our chronological life, the rites in which we participate measure our movement along another line. This ego time, or time of self-fulfillment, marks the less regular but still inevitable inner growth of the person. It becomes part of our personal history. After the rite of passage, one is changed forever. As we age, as we deepen in our spiritual path, as we pass these way stations and mark them, we join a time stream larger than our individual lives. There is first the time of our people, whoever they may be. The rite attunes us not just within our individual psyches but also coordinates our personal rhythms with the rhythm of our group. When William S. Condon first coined the term *entrainment*, he meant it to signify "the process that occurs when two or more people become engaged in each other's rhythms, when they synchronize."[13] This interpersonal synchrony, the rhythm between and among a people, is highly complex, consisting of body cues, distinctive musical rhythms, touching, and gestures that vary from culture to culture but always form powerful social binders. In a ritual of incorporation, one is brought into synchrony with others like oneself in a multilayered, intense, and holistic way. Like play (and there is always an aspect of "as if" in ritual), rites allow us to step outside the usual laws of time, to suspend all the normal rules and hierarchies, and then to reorganize our selves. With the support of the group, we move from step to step along the life line. With the validation of the group, we receive the courage to go on in our faith. Our worship group, at its best, forms a support system that helps us recognize the "fullness of time," when time is ripe for change.

In this way, the spiritual path allows for continual expansion through one's life. At its best, it works as a form of psychotherapy. The process of psychoanalysis consists of moving traumas out of the timeless and repetitive realm of the unconscious, where they arrived by repression, and to make them conscious, putting them in their proper place in the stream of time (the past) so that growth and development can resume and the person may have a future. Rituals of penance or baptism can be powerful means of reconstituting the self, of freeing oneself from one's past life and getting on with a future.

This may happen because of ritual's unique liminal nature, its ability to put us in sacred time. Being simultaneously in time and yet out of it, sacred time enables growth to happen. The duration and process of the ritual touches those timeless, healing places within us and within the world. "Without time, no working through can take place and repetition compulsion becomes the hallmark of the unconscious psychic functioning that at the conscious level may appear as obsessional pathology."[14] But rituals allow time to pass and encourage a "natural succession of events to allow growth, development and evolution."[15] By their nature, rituals help us access the unconscious realm that contains what Jung called "absolute knowledge," so called because it seems impersonal and detached from consciousness. Entering this primordial time dimension through ritual gives us access to a rich world that we normally only enter in dream or ecstasy or intoxication.[16] The rituals of passage, which embody the wisdom of our tribe, help us into and out of that realm.

As we grow in this faith journey, our comprehension of time increases. As a social entrainment process, ritual ties us to a group, and our time becomes one with the group's time. If ritual serves a progressive function in helping us grow into the future, it also serves a conservative function in preserving the past. We want to pass the forms on to the next generation; we become concerned about their survival into the future. This is Erik Erikson's generativity, concern for our progeny. But ritual always points beyond the tribe to the universe itself. When ritual is functioning well, we become capable of comprehending a larger past and future than that of our own group. Our knowledge of the passage of our own life gives us existential knowledge of time's passing, but a ritual tradition gives us an experience of timelessness. One learns to believe in permanence in spite of all, the permanence of life, of the universe, of the energy that drives it. One learns that one's life extends back into the origin of things, the cosmogon, and into the end of things, the eschaton. One learns how one fits into the flow of all time, and learns to move in rhythm with the universe itself.

Thus, liturgy and ritual stitch together the individual's life and entrain it to the life of our community, and then beyond that to the lives of all other human beings who also seek the timeless places within and outside themselves, and finally to the life span of the universe itself. In the end, religion is not an opiate, as Karl Marx held, but a stimulant, stimulating us to expanded consciousness of our place in the world.

By now, it should be obvious that the consequences of trying to live without religious experience are grave for both an individual and a culture. If states of religious ecstasy in fact provide us with opportunities for expanding human consciousness in a unique way, then attempting to live a purely secular, humanistic life cuts us off from one of the most powerful tools for cultural and perhaps even psychological growth ever contrived. As Arnold Toynbee pointed out, the world's great religious traditions were not simply by-products of cultures, they were, in fact, the very foundation of those cultures. Spiritual processes had material consequences and manifested themselves in the great civilizations of the Nile and Tigris and Euphrates River Valleys, in the Attic civilization of ancient Greece, and in the flowering of the Christian Middle Ages and Renaissance.

But if the religious experience of sacred time is so important, then why did we, as a culture, let it go? Why did we decide to ignore sacred time altogether and instead give ourselves over fully to clock time? To find an answer to this question, we must go back two thousand years into our culture's past.

Our coming to a purely secular understanding of time was the result of a cultural development that took centuries, and to comprehend it fully we will have to return to the earliest days of the Christian era and retrace the steps our culture took as it moved away from a sense of sacred time. If we are to live our way back into a relationship with eternity, we need to understand how and when that relationship slipped away.

CHAPTER 4

Books of Hours

WE HAVE BECOME so clock dominated, so much in thrall to our experience of secular time, that it is easy to forget that time and eternity were not always so far from each other. Once they participated in an intricate dance. Today we take the notion of a tightly scheduled life for granted, so much so that we feel we have no time for the sacred. If we hope to regain a sense of sacred time, we need to understand when and how sacred time got divorced from clock time. It is a fairly recent phenomenon.

Thirty-some years ago, a friend of mine became a Roman Catholic nun. She was given a leather-bound prayer book containing her daily devotions. She carried this book with her everywhere, and at prescribed hours she undid its clasp, opened the book, and recited the devotions appropriate to the day and time. In those days, all nuns and priests carried such books for their daily prayers. Today she is still a nun, but she is also a college professor, and she carries another book: her daily planner. Like her book of canonical hours, this one is fancily bound and has an impressive clasp, but there the likeness ends.

Her old book of daily prayers ensured that several times a day she would turn her thoughts away from this time-bound vale of tears and address those parts of her life that were timeless. Her daily planner, on the other hand, points to nothing beyond itself except work, duty, and the next committee meeting. The one was a source of peace, the other of feeling frazzled.

Once upon a time, the wealthy and the powerful carried books of hours as signs of their devotion. To carry such a book was to display status, prestige, and reverence. When medieval and Renaissance nobility had their portraits painted, they chose to show themselves clasping those books, their fingers perhaps tucked into a page as if they had just been interrupted from an intimate colloquy with God. Along with their jewels, their family coats of arms, and the quality of their cloaks, their books of hours were signs of their social standing as well as symbols of their devotion to God. Today, executives would likely never be seen with a prayer book, yet they would feel somehow undressed without their modern "books of hours." These books, either the paper or the computerized kind, send many of the same signals as their medieval counterparts did.

People treat their daily planners the way monks and nuns used to treat their prayer books. They keep them close at all times. They clasp them with missionary zeal as they head from meeting to meeting. With long-range and short-range plans, people plot out their workplace eschatology. The planner in today's society carries much mana, or spiritual power, and forgetting one's planner is a major sin of omission. Like medieval displays of conspicuous piety, the planner announces to the world that you are one whose life and time are worth something. The jewel-encrusted covers of medieval psalm books and the ornately illuminated pages of the Lindisfarne Gospels announced the value and importance of their books' contents. The sober leatherette of the daily planner, as plain as the binding of a King James Bible, holds lists of engagements no less valuable to us than the word of God was to the ancients.

The parallels between religious books of hours and our contemporary ones reflect our respective sets of values. While the intricate Celtic knots of the Book of Kells invited us to contemplate the interrelationship between the world of time and the world of eternity, the various interactive sections of the modern planner show only the interweaving of the various clock-bound schedules that make up the fabric of our contemporary lives. The Bible contained prophecies of the distant future, but the planner's prophecy consists only of this week's engagements, meticulously penciled in, which merely fulfill last week's commitments of where to be at a particular time. The alphabetized lists of phone numbers and e-mail addresses are arrayed like the genealogies of the elders of Zion; the brief almanacs and conversion tables are like synoptic texts guiding you through the valley of the shadow of international business travel; and in the back reaches of the volume, like the Book of Revelation, is stored the apocalyptic vision of the five-year plan. Yet none of this points beyond our horizontal realm to the vertical realm in which we also live.

It is thoroughly ironic, therefore, that our modern books of hours actually had their beginnings in early monasticism. The whole business of scheduling, which today seems to keep us from gaining access to sacred time, originated in the regimen of early Christian monks who organized their daily routine of work and prayer according to canonical hours, which were signaled by the ringing of a bell. Scheduling actually began as a way of keeping one's attention focused on eternity, and only gradually did it become an end in itself. The journey was long and complex, but it is worth retracing in detail as we attempt to find out just how a sense of sacred time slipped from our grasp. In the medieval sense of time, we may even find a model for ourselves, for in their premodern view we can observe a profound integration of sacred and profane time, a delicate balance of time and eternity. The story begins with people who, like many modern people, wanted to get away from their busy lives in order to pray.

In the early years of the Christian era, the Roman empire was collapsing. Barbarian tribes were pressing down from the north, and life was generally chaotic compared to the relatively ordered Roman world that had just faded. As the Christian religion emerged to replace classical mythology, it took on a number of forms, and almost from the start, an ascetic strain seems to have manifested itself. St. Ignatius of Antioch notes that as early as 110 C.E. at Smyrna there was a group of people who voluntarily withdrew from the world to assume lives of chastity and abstinence. They practiced lives of prayer and devotion, usually in their own homes or those of parents or relatives. It was a private practice, involving fasting two days a week and praying at the third, sixth, and ninth hours to commemorate the hours traditionally assigned to the condemnation, crucifixion, and death of Jesus. Each week these hermits gathered for a night-long vigil of readings, chants, and hymns to bring in the Sabbath. This lifestyle, with its set daily devotions and communal meetings, is the obvious ancestor of what eventually became the divine office of the later monks.

The acknowledged "father of monasticism" was St. Anthony, born about 251 C.E. in Egypt. A hermit and anchorite, he withdrew from the world into the desert to devote himself to a life of solitary prayer. Soon, however, word got out, and so many people came to him in the desert that small villages began to form around him. The followers lived by no single rule or communal lifestyle. As paradoxical as an anarchists' convention, these early communities were composed of solitaries who nonetheless wanted to live in fairly close quarters. Each followed his or her own daily regimen, bound only by the common experience of being near Anthony. Life in this sacred community must have been fairly chaotic, with so many so-called solitaries bunched together with little or no communal organization. Eventually, some sort of order had to be found that would allow them to keep their focus on God.

The first true community of monks (ironically, the word *monk* is derived from the Greek *mono*, meaning one who lives alone) was founded by a Roman soldier turned ascetic named Pachomius (286–346 C.E.). In a small community along the Nile, Pachomius directed a group that lived according to a common rule. In addition to the poverty and chastity assumed by previous ascetics, the followers of Pachomius also pledged obedience, perhaps inspired by Pachomius's military career. It was Pachomius who seems to have instituted the idea of a common daily schedule to keep some order in the community. The regimen consisted of prayers at dawn, noon, sundown, and midnight and twice-weekly sessions of common spiritual instructions under the direction of the community's leader. By Pachomius's death in 346, several monasteries had been opened on this same principle, and by the early fifth century the monastic lifestyle had spread to Italy, Gaul (at Tours and Lerins), and Ireland (St. Patrick arrived 420–430 C.E.).

The monastic life must have been attractive to people living in those unsettled times. Throughout the collapsed Roman empire, bloody battles for control raged. Odoacer, a German who seized control of Rome in 476, effectively put an end to the empire as Roman. Theodoric, a Goth, ruled

493–526 in spite of a bloody but unsuccessful attempt to reunify the empire by the Eastern emperor Justinian. It was a time of general upheaval and uncertainty.

In the midst of all this confusion, Benedict of Nursia (c. 480–c. 547) finally gave form to monasticism as we know it, and it was his famous rule that became the direct ancestor of the modern-day planner.[1] Like Anthony before him, Benedict attempted to retire from the social chaos of his time. Taking refuge in a cave at Subiaco, he tried to live the life of an ascetic, but, as had happened to Anthony in the desert, followers came. Benedict fled Subiaco and took up solitary residence at Monte Cassino, near the town of Cassium, which had been left impoverished by the conflicts of the previous half century, but the would-be hermit was once again besieged by followers. In the end, he realized he had to give up the search for solitude and, as a compromise, founded a monastic community for which he wrote his famous *Regula Monachorum*, now known as *The Rule of St. Benedict*. It is a fascinating document that has governed the way monks have lived, worked, eaten, and prayed for the past fifteen hundred years, and in it Benedict crafted a way of life in which sacred time could interact with secular time in an exquisite balance.

Central to the whole scheme is a regular schedule of *horae*, or hours, at which the monks perform certain jobs, eat, or, most important, pray. The life was austere. In the middle of the night, a bell rang and the monks, who slept in their clothes on straw mattresses in a dormitory, rose silently for the ninety-minute prayers known as Vigils. Following this, still in darkness, they practiced *meditatio*, during which they memorized the Psalter or lessons until Matins (morning prayer), which consisted of a half-hour's worth of readings from Scripture, and prayers. After this, they spent three hours in *lectio divina*, reading either from the Bible or from the church fathers. Psalms were chanted for the prayer time known as Prime, immediately after dawn, which was followed by Terce, the third hour after dawn. After Terce the monks paid attention to their worldly needs, performing manual labor in the fields. (Later in history, they would also work in *scriptoria*.) At midday they convened for Sext and in midafternoon for None. After None, literally the ninth hour after dawn, the monks had their first meal of the day, listening in silence to a sacred reading. After dinner, the monks read until Vespers, which began about half an hour before sunset. After this, a short period of open time, perhaps for recreation, was assigned, and the day finally ended with Compline, after which the monks returned to their straw mats for a few hours' sleep before the Vigils bell rang to begin the cycle again.

Thus, the rules of St. Benedict governed virtually every minute of the monks' day. Despite the apparent regularity and regimentation, however, they were still some distance from our modern sense of a schedule. For starters, The Rule was surprisingly flexible. The hours of the original *horae canonicae* were not regular sixty-minute hours, so our sense of time coming at us like empty bottles on an assembly line was not part of their sense of time. There were no clocks in the earliest days of the monasteries to measure out identical hours. Rather, the length of the early Benedictine "hour" was variable, arrived at by dividing the hours of daylight and the hours of darkness into twelve parts each, much like the ancient Egyptian and Roman systems.

As a result, these hours were not mechanical and regimented. They fell at different times of day depending on the time of year. The very names of the canonical hours were derived from their distance from sunrise, and so they maintained a close connection to the natural cycle of day and night. Prime was prayed at sunrise, Terce three hours after sunrise, Sext six hours after, None nine hours after.[2] Because time was calculated by dividing the hours of daylight by twelve, a monk's hour in summer was significantly longer than an hour in winter. In fact, the twelve hours of daylight, the *horae temporales*, were equal to sixty-minute hours only twice a year, on the equinoxes. As a result, the prayer hours would be at a slightly different time every day. Similarly, bedtimes and rising times were tied to the rising and setting of the sun. Living by sun time rather than clock time, the monk experienced the day as longer or shorter depending on the season. *The Rule of St. Benedict* takes this into account, allowing for three different timetables through the year, one each for winter, summer, and the liturgical season of Lent. The long nights of winter meant that the monks got some extra sleep at night, and on the long days of summer The Rule provided for a two-hour nap in the afternoon.

Our modern hour, by contrast, is inflexible from season to season, formed of exactly sixty minutes ticked off with regularity. Our workday, lacking the flexibility and responsiveness of the ancient hours, is always of the same duration, week in and week out. The result may be a sense of being on a treadmill, our lives stretched on the procrustean bed of the clock.

Conversely, there is comfort in the order and regularity of *The Rule of St. Benedict*. Even though every moment of the day seems accounted for, there is not much sense of hurry about it. We sense that there was a different rhythm of life in the monastery and in the Middle Ages generally than in the modern world, one more in tune with the seasons of the year, the rhythm of the liturgy, and the pulse of the lower psychological regions. We can hear this flexible rhythm in the liquid melisma of chant sung by the ancient monks. Sung properly, Gregorian chant is not mensural and rhythmically exact. The beat of modern music is metronomic, with each rhythmic interval taking exactly the same amount of time. Chant, on the other hand, has uneven rhythmic dynamics when properly sung. (Often modern singers who attempt to sing Gregorian chant will try to make its rhythm like modern rhythm, and the attempts usually fall flat somehow.) When we listen to monks like the Benedictine Monks of Santo Domingo de Silos who have maintained the living tradition of ancient chant (and who had a couple of smash CDs a few years ago), we hear the rhythmic variability originally intended. The tempo slows down and speeds up subtly to emphasize text and dynamics. A group of singers, by virtue of living together, can intuitively respond to subtle changes in rhythm in an organic rather than a mechanical way. This skill comes out of a lived experience rather than a learned technique. The monks share the same time sense, in their daily regimen and in their music.

Just as the tempo of monastic music varied, the length of an hour of prayer in the ancient Benedictine monastery varied as well. Without a clock, the hour was told by the saying of a certain number of prayers, variable depending on the time of the liturgical year. The hour of Terce, for example, might be told by the length of time it took to sing five psalms for the dead. Obviously the hour could be longer or shorter depending on the tempo of the singers and the number and length of the prayers prescribed.

Similarly, the daily schedule was not as rigid as it first appears. It followed the rhythm of the liturgical year, changing from season to season. The dynamic shape of the liturgical year gave movement and variation to the calendar year, speeding it up and slowing it down. By following the liturgical year, the individual and community attuned themselves to the larger temporal rhythms of the seasons and, more important, to the eternal rhythms of salvation. The four Sundays of Advent led to Christmas in such a way that the birth of Christ, the light prophesied by the Old Testament, neatly coincided with the winter solstice and the return of longer hours of daylight. Since the hours of Prime and Vespers were determined by sunrise and sunset, the monks could not help noticing the coincidence of the liturgical and natural seasons at every level of their lives. After Christmas came the feasts of the Circumcision (January 1), Epiphany (January 6), and Candlemas (February 2) in quick succession, followed by the long season of Lent, forty days of fasting and abstinence corresponding to the dearth of winter. During Lent, the darkest and dreariest time of year, the monks' daily chants and psalms focused on spiritual desolation: "Out of the depths, I cry to you, O Lord." But then, as the earth began to renew itself, the high drama of the Holy Week liturgies helped the monks relive and celebrate the core mystery of the Christian faith: Resurrection. The intense period from Palm Sunday through Good Friday, Holy Saturday, and Easter led, fifty days later, to the promise of Pentecost. Thus, from Advent through Pentecost, there was a quickening of time as the high holy days followed close on one another like the quickening pace of an intense passage of chant. From there the liturgical year passed into Ordinary Time, when the pace slowed, yet even during those long summer and early autumn months each day would be dedicated to some saint or mystery of the Christian faith, and the near-forgotten feast days we encounter in medieval literature—Michaelmas, Lammastide, Whitsunday, St. John's Eve—were each celebrated by believers.

The brilliance of the Benedictine schedule was perhaps the reason the Benedictine way of life spread so widely and quickly. It established a fine balance between time and eternity. The daily plan laid out in The Rule allowed the monk to keep his attention on God without having to worry about what needed doing next. The day unfolded in a formal but not rigid way, and the liturgical year carried him through cycles of death and rebirth year after year in a reassuring pattern.

Though it was structured to leave nary an idle moment, the monk's day remained focused on timeless eternity. The regular chanting of the liturgical hours kept the monks' attention on God, and even in periods of manual labor and silence they were encouraged to keep one part of their consciousness in eternity. *Laborare et orare.* Benedict encouraged activity and discouraged idleness, a characteristic of monastic life also seen in modern times, but, in contrast to the harried yuppie's, all of the monk's activities were to be spiritually focused. The mundane duties of daily life in the Middle Ages existed in a sacred context. The end and purpose of all the acts of life was eternal joy in heaven. The distinctive medieval attitude about time that resulted from this belief was quite different from our own. The Benedictine monk, in spite of the regimentation of his daily life, seems to have possessed an attitude that scholar Ricardo Quiñones called "temporal nonchalance." Even though their lives were short compared to ours, our medieval ancestors seemed much less concerned with the passage of time. Quiñones writes, "For the Middle Ages time could be abundant, because behind the chances and changes of events, man could sense a higher directing order . . . his beginnings and his ends were in the hands of a providential and concerned divinity. Because of his faith he could then exist in an attitude of temporal ease."[3] Temporal ease. What a far cry from our contemporary sense of time famine. This was an age when people could begin building cathedrals, knowing full well that no individual alive at the beginning of construction would live to see the end. Yet they also did not care, for the two hundred or three hundred years it might take to complete the building was but a moment compared to the eternity each person would live. All of that, of course, would change, but for a historical moment a balance was achieved.

Perhaps the last gasp of the medieval sense of time is found in the flowering of the lavishly illustrated books of hours so prized by the late medieval nobility. They reflect an attitude toward life that we have mostly lost in our mad rush. Medieval books of hours were not daily planners in our modern sense. They were private prayer books for the laity loosely modeled on those used by the clergy. Books of hours varied somewhat in content, length, and arrangement, but they all contained at least a calendar that listed feasts and saints' days. In the Middle Ages, these feasts could be considerable. Every day in the church calendar was devoted to some saint or other, and special days were marked in red. Also included in a typical book of hours were excerpts from the Gospels, and various offices of the Virgin, prayers for the dead, psalms, and litanies of the saints that people could refer to as needed.

Today we see these books only under glass in museums or rare-book rooms like the one at the Vatican library. In their time, however, they were living documents. Their calendars, prayers, and meditations gave form to the dynamic interweaving of time and eternity. They are worth further study if we are to move closer to an understanding of sacred time, for they were "soul guides," taking their users on a spiritual journey through life and into eternity.

Medieval books of hours cannot be read the way we read books in the information age, going through them from start to stop, efficiently extracting information. For starters, they were handwritten in elegant scripts with highly ornate capitals and ornamental ascenders and descenders. Decoding the text took time. The books are often filled with brilliant illuminations that interact with the text. Some are central to the page while others fill the margins. Sometimes they are charming, sometimes grotesque. Sometimes they are related to the text on the page, more often not. The complex layout shows that our medieval ancestors invented intertextuality long before postmodernism thought of the term. As a result, the reader had to carry on a discourse with the page. The word *discourse* means to run around, and reading a book of hours required the reader to take time to let his or her eyes play over the page, meditating on the interplay of words and images, text and decoration, the sacred and the profane. The reader had to meditate on the characters in the sinuous vines of the margins or in the historiated capitals, figure out the relation between the illuminated scenes of Christ's passion and death and the text. What did it mean that while the sacred mysteries transpired in the center of the page, characters in the margins (characters like us, after all) got on with their weaving, spinning, and the general play of life? Here was displayed for the eye to see all the complex interweaving of time and eternity.

Spending even an hour or two with the exuberant profusion that one encounters on the pages of medieval books of hours, we can imbibe a sense of what was once called "the fullness of time," the sort of delightful and poised mixture of the sacred and the profane (even sometimes the obscene) that would later send Puritans or hard-shell Baptists into spasms of rage. But this was a time mode with which the Middle

Ages seemed quite at ease. There was no apparent contradiction between sacred and secular time, only a complex interweaving.

In the beautiful *Heures de Jeanne d'Evreux*, created circa 1325 by the artist Jean Pucelle for the wife of Charles V of France, the sacred texts are surrounded by whimsical scenes. In the margins, one encounters two men riding goats who tilt at a barrel mounted on a post, or a beggar woman seated in a corner. Servants carry bathwater, monsters play reed pipes, knights in armor ridiculously stalk rabbits. Acrobats with dancing dogs perform in the margin below the illumination of the birth of Christ, monkeys climb up the lines of Scripture, humans battle basilisks, and so on until the final "Amen" on the last page, where a rabbit and a monster perch side by side. Time and eternity played together.

"The medieval man had time for play and fun," James J. Rorimer, former director of the Metropolitan Museum of Art writes in his introduction to the facsimile edition of *The Hours of Jeanne d'Evreux*. "If there were to be outlets for humor, a private prayer book was a place for the whimsy of the imaginative artist."[4]

To read a book of hours was to take full delight in the world of time and the world of eternity. There was no sense of having to "move on," as we might have in a modern book. The reader could pray from the text prescribed for the appropriate day and hour, or meditate on the illustration of the miracles of St. Louis healing the blind or feeding lepers, or follow the marginal adventures of a hawking party on the saint's calendar page for May, or perhaps spend time watching four women play a popular medieval game called "frog in the middle" directly below the illustration for the Annunciation.

In these books of hours, we get a sense that people in the

Middle Ages took the time, or simply had the time, to delight in life. How often in modern life do we hear people say,
too late, they wished they had taken time to smell the roses?
In a book of hours created for Engelbert of Nassau in the late
fourteenth century by an artist known only as the Master of
Mary of Burgundy, we find evidence that people in less hurried times did exactly that. In beautiful trompe l'oeil, flowers
are strewn across gilt pages. Eye-fooling bees and butterflies
suck nectar from pansies and columbine, and so life went on
in a leisurely way with a sacred mystery at its core. In the
Middle Ages they had a term for this abundance and profusion of life, *natur naturans*, "nature naturing," the world going
about its regular business without hurrying, in a relaxed
rhythm, in the fullness of time. Would that we had time for
such beauty.

It's true, of course, that books of hours were created for the
nobility, and a modern reader might object that these people
had "time on their hands" because they had servants to do all
the work. As I will show in my chapter on telling time, however, the temporal nonchalance of the Middle Ages extended
down through the ladder of society to include the so-called
working classes.

Looking at medieval books of hours gives us a glimpse into
another sense of time, and perhaps no other book of hours
does this better than the *Très Riches Heures du Duc de Berry*, an
unfinished fifteenth-century text whose most famous illuminations were created by the immensely talented and sensitive
Limbourg brothers, Jean, Herman, and Pol. Like the great
Gothic cathedrals built earlier in the period, the book is a collective work, produced by the Limbourg brothers and the
many unknown artists who painted the tympana at the top of
each page, the calligraphers and rubricators, various work-

shop artists, and the painter Jean Colombe, who took up the work some sixty-nine years after the Limbourg brothers and, like them, left it unfinished.[5]

The book is worth examining at some length. The *Très Riches Heures* is a large and complex book, consisting of 206 folio pages, 300 by 215 millimeters each, gathered into thirty-one quires. One of a kind, it is arguably the most valuable book in the world, and it is kept in the Bibliothèque of the Musée Condé in Chantilly, France.[6] It is an exquisite object of visual art, but its real subject is time and eternity. In some ways, it is even a visual summa of the medieval understanding of the proper relationship between time and eternity.

The first (and most famous) part of the *Très Riches Heures* consists of a calendar of the months of the year with accompanying illustrations. The first major illustration is a narrative painting of the fall of Adam and Eve. It shows the beginning of time as we understand it. Reading from left to right, we see the serpent tempting Eve, Eve offering the apple to Adam, God ordering them expelled from the garden, and the cherubim escorting them out the gate in wearing fig leaves. Because the *Très Riches Heures* is an elaborate calendar as well as a book of hours, we may interpret this initial illustration as the story of how we fell from the timeless world of Eden into the world of time that we inhabit. We all know the story: Adam and Eve are expelled into a world of suffering. When we turn the page to January, however, we are greeted not with a scene of death and punishment but with the image of a lavish winter feast presided over by the Duc de Berry himself. It is an astonishing image of the postlapsarian world as a kind of demi-Eden created not by God but by human art. The fig leaves of Adam and Eve have become the sumptuous clothes of court, and here, in the duke's midwinter feast, nature's bounty is celebrated. Though it is a cold world outside, indoors the fireplace is blazing, our friends gather around us, and exotic hounds wander through the hall delicately nipping up the bits of food we let fall. O *felix culpa* indeed if this is the world we have been exiled to!

We are never allowed to forget, however, that time passes. Across from this lavish illustration of earthly splendor is the gilt and gaily colored calendar page for January, so we can keep track of time. Each day is assigned its saint or feast, with special days like January 6 highlighted in red ink, the original red-letter days. In addition, the calendar pages of the *Très Riches Heures* contain much more information related to the world of time. Each page notes solar and lunar days and contains a "Golden Number" that reconciles the solar and lunar years by referring to the so-called Metonic cycle of nineteen years. Each leaf shows the length of time between sunrise and sunset at the latitude of Paris and indicates the old Roman divisions of the month into Nones, Ides, and Kalends. At the top of every illustrated page is a deep-blue tympanum, or half circle, which depicts the thirty degrees of the zodiac visible that month as well as concentric bands that show, in ascending order, the Arabic numerals for the days of the month, a letter of the alphabet that corresponds to the Golden Number, indicators of the phases of the moon, the name of the month, the pictorial symbol of the zodiac houses visible that month, and the thirty or thirty-one days of the month repeated. In the center of each tympanum is an identical image of a sun god, seated on a mansion mounted on wheels and holding the burning orb of the sun as he is pulled through the sky by two fiery horses.

There is, in other words, a huge amount of calendric information surrounding the illuminations for each month. That and the saints' days on the opposing pages serve to remind us that this world of passing time exists, in all its complexity, in the context of eternity. The layout of the page might almost be a *memento mori*, but there is nothing in it of contempt for the world. Rather, as one turns from month to month, one marvels at the beauty and order of this world of time where each season has its proper activity, pleasure, and beauty and where the saints' days and the holy feasts exist in perfect synchrony. Even after four hundred years, the book continues to astonish and delight with its images of grace and civilization and the orderly unfolding of time.

In February, we see women lifting their skirts to warm their legs by the fire while outside a man chops wood as the beehives sleep beneath caps of snow. Black rooks nibble on seed in a barnyard while sheep huddle in a croft. All is as it should be in the coldest season of the year.

In March, the hard earth yields to the plow and ox. Workers prune the winter kill from the vine stocks, and the last of the winter roots are harvested. The sheep that had been shivering in the croft now return to the fields. In the background, we see the château of Lusignan, one of many owned by the duke, and above its tower hovers a dragon.[7]

The illumination for April continues time's movement into full spring. It is a ravishing scene of *reverdi*, the regreening of the earth that forms such a strong theme in the poetry of the Middle Ages. It is the visual equivalent, perhaps, of the opening eighteen lines of Chaucer's *Canterbury Tales*, in which April, with her sweet showers, has broken through the dry crust of March and brought the earth to life again. In this painting, a betrothed couple, variously identified as the Duc de Berry's granddaughter Bonne d'Armagnac and Charles D'Orleans, engaged in 1410, or Marie de Berry and Jean de

Clermont, betrothed around 1400, are shown with the duke and his granddaughter as witnesses. It is a springtime idyll. The noble party stands outside the walls of the castle of Dourdan. The happy couple exchange rings, love being the proper business of springtime, while other members of the party admire the new growth, picking violets from the lawn. In the background, two fishing boats ply the waters in hopes of a bountiful catch. They are enjoying the world of time.

Probably the most famous painting in the book is the illustration for the month of May. A mixed party of men and women, young nobility by their garb, ride forth with garlands in their hair and around their necks, celebrating May with time-honored rites and pomp. Their green garments put them in sync with the season, and the small dogs that accompany them are not hunting dogs but domestic pets. Trumpets blare to welcome in May, and so the true beginning of the pleasant months of the year is marked.

In June, the peasants scythe and rake the hay. The figures move in perfect symmetry. The men's figures sweep back the scythes and mow in synchrony, almost like dancers. The buildings in the background, the Palais de la Cité and Ste. Chapelle, show that they are just outside Paris, and above, in the tympanum of the page, Gemini gives way to Cancer.

In July comes the harvest of the first wheat and sheep shearing near the Château de Clain in Poitiers. Peasants in straw hats and *petits draps* (drawers) perform their tasks without apparent haste. These are the months of summer fullness. In August, we see the nobility ride out on a hawking expedition, sparrow hawks and merlins on their gloved hands as beaters with sticks try to flush game. In the background, figures swim in the river behind Estampes, another de Berry possession. From the expressions of the characters, one could guess that the conversation in this mixed group of men and women is more likely to be amorous than about hunting, but then, as Chaucer shows us, the word venery in the Middle Ages had double meanings, related to both hunting and the goddess Venus.

The year rounds out as we head into September. In the foreground, the grape harvest is in full swing. Traffic heads into the castle, this time the Château de Saumur near Angers, storing provisions for the coming winter. But there is no sense of impending hardship. A male peasant leisurely enjoys one of the grapes from a cluster he's just picked. A woman peasant adjusts her headdress. A bull munches grass, and the donkeys laden with full grape baskets stand waiting. A woman with a loaded basket on her head slowly approaches the castle. Though this is a work scene, it feels calm, and everything in it unfolds without strain, as if they had all the time in the world.

October is seed time for the wheat, and as the old year winds down, a man on a horse pulls a harrow through the field, while another on foot scatters seed. A ragged scarecrow, posed as an archer, draws his bow to keep away the scavenging birds. And next comes November, where we see a swineherd leading pigs beneath oak trees, where he uses a long stick to knock down acorns for the pigs to eat, fattening them for the winter feast. Here we cannot help thinking of the great feast that started the year in January's calendar. The labors of the months have almost come full circle. Finally, in December, we see hunting dogs falling on a downed boar. The gray, dead earth and yellow-leafed trees dominate the foreground and middle ground.

But this is not the end. If the *Très Riches Heures* consisted only of the familiar calendar pages, it would still be an extraordinary work of art and a valuable window into the late medieval mind, but we need to remember that the calendar pages make up only the first few folios of this very long work. Where this first portion attracts us modern people with the earthly splendor of the Duc de Berry and his circle, the book is intended, after all, to be a religious book of hours, the calendars to remind us of saints' days. Beginning with folio 14v, therefore, the book takes a decided turn toward the religious and even the mystical. This portion is by far the larger, and it serves to put the twelve months of the year, with all the secular pleasures of the court, into an eternal context.

This latter section of the book begins with an enigmatic figure known as the Anatomical or Zodiacal Man. The nude figure of a long-limbed man with curled golden hair is painted frontally and with a mirror image of his back. He stands within a mandorla, in the borders of which is a calendar of the twelve months that also contains the twelve signs of the zodiac in their appropriate places. The zodiacal signs are also arranged on the figure from head to toe. Aries is at the top of his head, and the other signs follow in order until we find Pisces at his feet. Taurus the bull is draped around his neck, the Gemini, one male and one female, appear on each arm, Cancer is at the chest, and Leo between the nipples. Virgo is at the heart level and Libra over the stomach. Scorpio appears at the loins, Sagittarius at the thighs, Capricorn at the knees, and Aquarius at the calves. He is both man and universe.

According to scholar Harry Bober, this unusual figure is an anatomical diagram used to guide physicians in bloodletting. In this period, astrology and medicine were closely related, since the movements of the stars and planets were thought to govern the lives of human beings. To determine the best time to bleed a patient, one needed an accurate calendar of astronomical positions and also a guide to which signs governed various organs of the body. As Bober points out in a monograph study of the figure, "prognosis and treatment depended on the humoral constitution of the patient, the day of the moon at the commencement of the malady, and the relation of that 'planet' to the sign of the ailing member."[8] Perhaps it was bad science by modern standards, but it does reflect a holistic vision that we can appreciate and even envy. Macrocosm and microcosm interact on every level.

This extraordinarily beautiful and enigmatic image appears at the very center of the *Très Riches Heures*. The calendar of the year, with its reminders of the saints' days and its lavish illustrations, precedes it, and following it come readings from the Gospels, prayers to the Virgin, penitential psalms, and the office of the dead. The anatomical-zodiacal figure thus becomes the linchpin that connects the two parts of the book. The diagram is a dramatic visual statement of the medieval belief that the human being is the point where the opposites of macrocosm and microcosm, eternity and time, are reconciled. As Bober points out, the Limbourg brothers achieved an aesthetic and iconographic synthesis that transcends the rather crude figures of this *homo signorum* found in later printed texts. This figure, a rare fusion of meaning with beauty of form, encountered in the very middle of the book, provides a transition from the secular emphasis of the first thirteen folios to the purely religious focus of the remaining 187. Having reveled in the secular pleasures of the year, we now encounter this figure that leads our thoughts to the heavens.

Appropriately, the next folio (17) offers us the beginning of John's gospel and an illumination of John on Patmos seeing the vision of the Apocalypse. The illuminations in the rest of book are without exception religious and are closely related to the texts that face and surround them. The mode is apocalyptic, seeing beyond the veil of time into the world of eternity. Prayers to the Virgin are illuminated with an image inspired by the Book of Revelation (12:1): "A woman clothed with the sun and moon under her feet." Folio 25 again illustrates the Fall in four scenes, but this time the image is not followed by the luxurious life at the court of Duc de Berry but rather by the Annunciation (folio 26), a visual reminder that the new woman, Mary, redeems the sin of the first woman, Eve.

Other images and prayers follow. The Psalms are accompanied by images of King David and other Old Testament scenes, as well as allegories such as depictions of the mystical marriage of Christ and the church. The Penitential Psalms are illuminated by the fall of the rebel angels, and the prayers of the office of the dead offer us horrific and graphic images of hell. One in particular (folio 108) stands out as a contrast to the lavish life depicted in the first folios of the *Très Riches Heures*. Satan lies on his back on a bed of red-hot coals, blowing souls upward in the fiery column of his breath. Around him, demons torture other souls, fanning the flames beneath Satan with large bellows. Among the sinners, we find many clerics, as if to remind us that no one is exempt from God's judgment. The book ends with a compilation of the masses for the liturgical year, beginning with Christmas.

And now perhaps we are ready to return to the contrast between the ancient books of hours and our own. If they are read and prayed in conjunction with the flow of the liturgical year, the *Très Riches Heures du Duc de Berry* and other medieval books of hours form in the mind a unified and grand narrative. As they meditated on the feast days in the calendar section, followed the year through the masses toward the end, prayed the various offices, and allowed their imaginations to be stirred by visions of paradise and the terrors of hell, the owners of these books of hours would be reminded several times a day of the great narrative cycle of history, from Creation through the Apocalypse, and their own place in it. Books of hours would encourage and help them to live their lives *sub specie aeternitatis*. How different from our own books of hours, which only make us hurry more and pay less heed to eternity than we otherwise would!

The modern mind remains skeptical. Are we simply idealizing a time gone by? Hasn't human life always been lived in a rush, raging against an ever-dwindling allotment of time? Weren't the illustrations in the medieval books of hours idylls even then? Perhaps, but when I look at portraits of people of this period, their fingers tucked into their books of hours, they look back at me across the centuries as if I had just momentarily interrupted their reading. They do not appear anxious to get back to their books. They know there will be time. Their expression is most unlike that of the modern executive who looks in an irritated way at his planner to see if he can squeeze you in.

Perhaps we need to revive these ancient books of hours, books not meant to keep us on the fast track but meant to be read slowly, discursively, with an eye toward eternity. In medieval illuminations of the Annunciation, Mary is almost invariably shown holding a book of hours, looking up from her slow, perhaps even playful reading to see the angel Gabriel descending to tell her she is to be the mother of God. Who knows what visitations might come to us if we traded in our daily planners for ancient books of hours?

It is difficult today to remember that monks invented schedules to keep their minds on eternity rather than time.

What happened? How did the flexible medieval sense of time bring forth the time-obsessed modern man and woman? There is, of course, no simple answer, but essentially we might say our current obsession with time began with a simple problem the monks faced and with the ingenious but far-reaching solution they came up with.

The problem, of course, was that *The Rule of St. Benedict* called for the monks to rise in the so-called middle of the night. But how could they be sure they were rising at the proper hour? How does one determine the middle of a variable period between sunset and sunrise? Timekeeping became a major concern of the monastic community. In fact, it was what we might call an executive-level function, assigned by The Rule to the abbot himself or someone whom he personally designated.

The early monks tried a variety of ways to measure time accurately at night. From the beginning, one monk was assigned the task of staying awake to keep track of the time either by watching the stars, turning an hourglass, using a water clock, counting off the marks on a special candle, or reciting a certain number of prayers until it was the hour to wake the other brothers for Vigil. Each of these methods had its limits, of course. On cloudy nights, time could not be told by the stars, and water clocks worked well in the summer but froze in the winter. And all of these methods suffered from the same fundamental flaw: human frailty. While a brother's spirit may have been willing, his flesh, alas, was weak, and all too often the monk whose job it was to ring the clock at the appointed hour fell asleep and threw the whole monastery off schedule. This was no small matter in a community containing up to 120 monks and perhaps 175 attendant serfs in up to forty buildings. Often two monks were assigned the night watch in the hope that they could keep each other awake, but this didn't always work either.

Finally, sometime around the year 1200, the Benedictine monks solved the problem. They developed a verge-and-foliot escapement system, attached this via a set of gears to a round dial with hour markers on it, then connected these works to a bell-ringing mechanism, and thus the first clock was born.[9] Like most revolutionary ideas, it was simple at first. The first clocks needed no hands, for the monks only needed to know when the hour began, and the ringing bell sufficed for that. After the bell, the services and activities of the traditional horarium, Matins, Prime, Terce, and so on, would determine the duration of the "hour." But, even though this new system of timekeeping was flexible compared to our modern standards, it was not as flexible as it had been, and it quickly grew more rigid. Eventually, the ending of a canonical hour was no longer determined by when the monks got through the prayers assigned for that hour, but rather by the beginning of the next clock hour. Subtly, the servant was becoming the master, and eventually the hour became a fixed unit rather than a flexible one. A face and an hour hand were added to the mechanism. With the invention of mechanical clocks, an hour was always the same, day and night, winter and summer. The flexible, fluid, dynamic rhythm of the chant was being replaced by the steady beat of the metronome.

There had always been a prejudice against free time in the Benedictine rule. "Idleness is the enemy of the soul," states The Rule. "Therefore, at given times the brethren ought to be occupied in manual labor, and again at other times in prayerful reading." One or two senior monks were appointed to patrol the monastery during free periods to see that nobody was idly chatting. If they found any idlers, they were to reprove them as often as necessary, and if a particular brother proved recalcitrant, he was to be punished and made an example of.

Even the sick or aged were to be given some kind of work to fill their time and keep them from idleness. Punishment often consisted of a kind of temporal segregation, the monk being forced to eat and pray alone, out of sync with the others. With the coming of the clock and the regular sixty-minute hour, time became an empty bottle to be filled.

Lateness had also long been a concern in the monasteries. Before the advent of the mechanical clock, however, lateness was difficult to judge. Tardiness was defined as arriving at Prime after, say, the Gloria or a certain psalm. In the monastery, punctuality had a moral dimension. To be late was not just an inconvenience to others who might be disturbed by your entrance, it was tantamount to a moral fault, a failing in the monastic vow of obedience, and an affront to God. Once the clock arrived to measure one's lateness more precisely, punctuality to clock time came to be seen as a virtue and tardiness, by the clock, as a vice.

By 1400, according to Quiñones, the influence of the clock had replaced the older way of reckoning time by the canonical hours of prayers with the new system of telling time by clock hours. Sociologist Eviatar Zerubavel comments, "The replacement of seasonably variable 'hours' . . . by durationally uniform hours . . . anchored in clock time alone was just one further step in the evolution from a naturally based temporal order to an artificial and conventional one."[10]

With their invention of the mechanical clock, the Benedictines became the first human community to devise a system of telling time not directly related to observable nature.

It is true, of course, that the round face of the clock was modeled after the face of the sundial, and the "clockwise" movement of the clock's hand copied the direction of the sun across the sky as viewed by someone in the Northern Hemisphere, but these connections with nature were and are quite abstract. They are not nearly as direct as watching the gnomon's shadow move across the face of a sundial or telling time by the position of the stars. The relationship between time and celestial motion or time and the change of seasons quickly became too abstract to be noticed anymore, and very subtly clock time came to have an existence of its own.

The rage for clocks quickly took hold of late medieval society, and elaborate and complex devices, like the astronomical clock in the cathedral at Strasbourg, were erected in public places. Eventually, clock time came to dominate civic life as clocks were mounted prominently on the main public squares, often smack in the middle of church facades so that, ironically, the church, which should have been a haven from the temporal world, became the building to which the community looked to learn the time. This architectural style came to seem quite normal even through the nineteenth century, so that the irony of seeing a clock mounted at the base of a spire was effectively blunted. Perhaps early on, church clocks even came to serve as reminders of death rather than eternity. An inscription beneath an old twelve-hour clock in the church of Santa Maria Novella in Florence concludes with this memento mori:

> . . . *whatever lingers on earth draws to its ebb.*
> *Alas the while! Time run by does not reverse its course.*
> *Alas, too near draws Mistress Death with her silent step.* [11]

This is a far cry from the "temporal nonchalance" of the earlier Middle Ages and the apparent ease with which time and eternity formerly coexisted. The sense of time expressed here is thoroughly modern, and the sentiment would fit well in our own books of hours. The age of the clock had begun.

CHAPTER 5

The Triumph of the Clock

AFTER TAKING hold in the monasteries, the clock quickly spread outside the convent walls. By 1309, the Church of St. Eustorgio in Milan boasted a clock. Other cities quickly followed: Beauvais in 1324; the Church of St. Gothard, Milan, in 1335; the monastery at Cluny in 1340. Chartres cathedral in 1359 boasted two clocks. By 1365, there were public clocks in Padua, Genoa, Bologna, and Ferrara.[1]

Most of these early clocks were in churches, but clocks quickly moved to public squares, and "community time" began to develop. European civic life began to march to a common beat. In 1370, Charles V of France installed clocks at his various palaces and ordered all other clocks in Paris to ring their bells at the same time as the royal clocks.[2]

The earliest clocks had no hands, only bells, but soon a single hand and a dial were added to tell the hours. The single hand went around the dial in the direction that would eventually become known as clockwise. Because of the clock's association with the movement of the planets (the sun was then considered a planet), medieval scholars and philosophers paid more attention to it than they did to other machines and even gave it preeminence. The gear mechanism used in clocks could also be used to build machines to copy the movements of the sun, moon, and planets. In 1271 a writer named Robert the Englishman wrote a book entitled *Sphere of Sacroboso*, which mentions clock makers of his day who were attempting to make an astronomical clock whose wheels would mimic the movements of the heavens and would utilize hanging weights to drive the mechanism. Elaborate and complex astronomical clocks began to appear in European cities surprisingly soon after the invention of the clock. Strasbourg's famous astronomical clock was built around 1350 and was immediately declared a wonder. It showed the movement of the planets and houses of the zodiac and also featured a procession of the three Magi before the Virgin and a crowing cock. Similar clocks appeared in Orvieto, Reggio, Wells, Lund (Sweden), Lübeck, and Berne. Most of these astronomical clocks showed the standard pre-Copernican universe, but in Bologna, a unique fifteenth-century astronomical clock showed the Pythagorean order, in which the sun and other planets circled a great ball of fire. (Strasbourg eventually added a post-Copernican movement.) A famous clock by Giovanni de Dondi, made around 1350 and surviving only in drawings and model form, showed movements of the sun, moon, and the five visible planets and even included elliptical gears to show the elliptical paths of the moon and Mercury. It is said to have taken de Dondi sixteen years to construct.

Cities vied with each other for the most complex and elaborate clocks. In many larger cities, like Venice, the clocks in the town squares, with their celestial mechanics and trumpeting angels, seemed to declare that this town is the very center of the universe.

During this time, naturally, the metaphor of the clockwork universe was born. The medieval scholar Nicholas Oresmus, or Nicole Oresme (d. 1382), seems to have been the first to view the universe as a God-made clock, but eventually Europeans as a group came to see the heavens themselves as a great machine and their maker a master artisan.[3] The clock that ran like the universe became the universe that ran like a clock.

Perhaps inevitably, this period also gave birth to an increasing number of sermons, tracts, and other literary references that emphasized the shortness of time. In Chaucer's *Canterbury Tales*, for example, the pilgrims' host Harry Bailey notes the angle of the sun, determines that the time is ten of the clock, and delivers a brief homily on not wasting time.

The medieval sense of temporal nonchalance was giving way to the fretting about time that became ever more prevalent in the Renaissance and after as telling time got more precise. By 1410, early spring-driven clocks were invented. The minute hand appeared more frequently in the sixteenth century, though it did not come into common use until the addition of the pendulum in the seventeenth century made clocks considerably more accurate, and by 1670 clocks with second hands were not unusual.[4]

The introduction of the clock into lay society in the fourteenth century led to some fascinating changes in the time sense of Europeans over the next few hundred years. As early as 1335, among textile workers, the hour began to be used as a unit of measuring work, replacing the old "day's work." While this may seem like a minor change, it reflects a refined sense of time as a commodity that can be broken down into smaller and smaller increments. Lewis Mumford notes that as the middle class arose in the Renaissance, "Time keeping passed into time-saving and time-accounting and time-rationing. As this took place, Eternity gradually ceased to serve as the measure and focus of human action."[5]

At the same time, a new sense of history arose, beginning

with the Renaissance, whose very name suggests that periods from the past must be recovered and reborn in the present. Prior to this, in the medieval conception of time, the "story" aspect of history was emphasized. The purpose of studying history was to teach us lessons about how to live in the present. The matter of chronology did not seem to matter much. In fact, by modern standards, many medieval historians were wildly inaccurate in their placing of events and their propensity for mingling the factual and fictional. But during the Renaissance, as Ricardo Quiñones recounts in *The Renaissance Discovery of Time*, clock time and historical time were redefined. The commercial enterprises of emerging capitalism, which involved the movement of goods, the rise and fall of market prices, the fluctuating value of money over time, and payment for hours of labor that could be more or less efficient depending on how the workers used their time, reinforced the importance of time and timing.

Not surprisingly, as this period went along, there were more references to time's passing and the need to save and preserve it. In sermons, new attention was paid to scriptural passages like Matthew 24, which in the parable of the ten bridesmaids admonishes us to be watchful, for we know not the day nor the hour, and to the parable of the talents, reinterpreted in a capitalistic sense to advise investors to use their money to make money over time, for opportunity will pass and soon it will be too late to make a good profit. Overall, as the next few centuries after the invention of the clock progressed, there was an "increased sense of urgency and a different emphasis on termination and final nothingness" compared with the classical and medieval acceptance of the comings and goings of time as a natural process.[6] The themes of *tempus fugit*, *memento mori*, and *carpe diem* became the stock-in-trade of later Renaissance poets and philosophers.

Early Renaissance humanists like Petrarch (1304–1374), and Leon Battista Alberti (1404–1472) ushered in this new sense of time and history with their studies of the classical world. The Renaissance writer Flavio Biondo (1392–1463) was apparently the first historian to divide the world up into the ancient, middle, and modern eras we still use today.[7] This division implies that we must reach back through time a great distance to recover a past that once existed but is now gone. Similarly, it cannot have escaped these humanists' notice that their era, too, would one day pass and become someone else's history, and this crucial historical consciousness of time's passing developed more and more as the centuries went on.

In reading Cicero's letters, which had been newly found in a manuscript in Verona in 1345, and other works of past great writers, Petrarch came to understand that history could be "made" by individuals interacting with the events of their time. For Petrarch and the others, the challenge presented by history was to "emulate" the past. The word *emulation* had a very specific meaning in the Renaissance. It was not simply a synonym for copying. Renaissance artists attempted first to match and then to surpass the works of the classical past. Men and women of talent could rise up and, if their timing was right, could achieve great and lasting monuments. Great art could be created, cities could be built, worlds could be conquered. The study of the past would become the means of building the future.

Historians Niccolo Machiavelli (1469–1527) and Francesco Guicciardini (1483–1540) wove this notion into their works. In *The Prince*, Machiavelli illustrates the working-out of what was implicit in Petrarch's notion of time and history. Strong personalities, with cunning and skill, could seize the opportunities time offered and cling tenaciously to power, at least for a while.

And there was the rub. Nothing lasted. There was no permanence. The study of ancient empires not only revealed possibilities for creating new worlds, it also provided clear and stark evidence that all things passed, that time ended all great empires, and that no individual, however powerful, could maintain his or her place forever. And as the medieval sense of living with one foot in eternity faded, a kind of anxiety about time set in. If one did not achieve greatness in this lifetime, then the opportunity was lost forever. Alfred von Marten, in his *Sociology of the Renaissance*, wrote, "after the fourteenth century the clocks in the Italian cities struck all the twenty-four hours of the day. It was realized that time was always short and hence valuable, that one had to husband it and use it economically if one wanted to become 'the master of all things.' Such an attitude had been unknown in the Middle Ages; to them time was plentiful and there was no need to look upon it as something precious. It became so only when regarded from the point of view of the individual who could think in terms of time measured out to him."[8]

Such an attitude had strange effects. Von Marten says that builders tried to find ever quicker methods of construction so buildings could be finished more swiftly. No more could people spend several generations building a cathedral, for time was short. Whitrow claims that time consciousness became so acute that the old *al fresco* method of painting on wet plaster was replaced by the *al secco* method of oil painting to save time. Petrarch himself, though living early in the period, scheduled himself with a fine time consciousness, allotting six hours a day for sleep, two for "other necessities," and the rest of the day for writing and study.[9] Leon Battista Alberti, too, had a daily *regola*, in which he rose each morning and charted out the things that had to be done that day so he could live his life *con ordine*, with order.[10] Though the Renaissance schedule was based on the medieval monks' daily hours, the emphasis shifted from sacred time to secular time.

Through the Renaissance, there was generally a sense of time's speeding up, of the rhythm of life getting quicker; and as the clock gained precision, the sense of time's passing more quickly accelerated. As clocks moved out of the public sphere and into the home, people began to regulate even their domestic lives as precisely as their public lives. By the sixteenth century, time consciousness had grown so fine and clocks had been made so precise that one could now actually be late by a matter of only minutes. In earlier times, appointments would be set for morning or for afternoon, or for such-and-such an hour, but, as Dr. Johnson noted in one of his *Rambler* essays, by the sixteenth century the Reformation leader Philip Melanchthon (1497–1560) was compelled to make very exact appointments, fixing both the hour and the minute so that he would not spend time waiting in idleness.

Late Renaissance writers like Shakespeare, Edmund Spenser, Ben Jonson, and others seem obsessed with time's passing, the shortness of life, and the imminence of death. In Shakespeare's early play *The Comedy of Errors*, a clock served as a plot device, marking the time by which all the strands of the farce had to be tidied up or poor old Egeon would lose his head. In his later plays, sonnets, and narrative poems, Shakespeare sometimes seemed obsessed to the point of depression with the devouring aspect of time. The final act of *Richard II* features the deposed king's soliloquy on time, and in it we can hear, brilliantly articulated, all the paradoxes of time, of which people in the Renaissance were excruciatingly aware. Richard sensed that the clock and the man had become one, and time and his life were running to their end simultaneously:

> *I wasted time, and now doth time waste me,*
> *For now hath time made me his numb'ring clock.*[11]

The Renaissance sense of time, timing, and history pervaded Shakespeare's chronicle plays, written in the 1590s. The tide of history moved forward, and some men, like Bolingbroke, his son Hal, and the Earl of Richmond rose to meet those events with exquisite timing, while others, like the Richards II and III faltered and failed. History moved on, and as the somber ending of *Henry V* reminded Shakespeare's audience, the achievements of one generation were often lost in the next.

In Shakespeare's later tragedies, written after 1600, the sense of time rushing inexorably forward was even greater. Watching *Macbeth*, one experiences an acceleration of time as the climax of the final battle approaches. Macbeth's thoughts, soliloquies, and dialogues are interrupted by a flow of events that seems, in the end, beyond his control. Macbeth's promised conversation with Banquo, put off in act 2, never occurs, and in the end, as his world collapses about him, Macbeth delivers his somber soliloquy on the apparently meaningless procession of tomorrows creeping forward senselessly "to the last syllable of recorded time."

In his narrative poem *The Rape of Lucrece*, Shakespeare gave vent to a long disquisition on time, which he addressed as "Misshapen time, copesmate [comrade] of ugly night" and "Eater of youth." As usual, Shakespeare was more troubled by the ravaging aspects of time than he was delighted by time's possibilities.

Shakespeare was hardly alone among Renaissance poets in

his obsession with time. Spenser too was highly aware of time's passing, and Ben Jonson ends his masque "Love Freed from Ignorance and Folly" (1611) with a reference to time in its guise as Chronos, who

> *Is eating every piece of hour*
> *Some object of rarest worth.*[12]

The medieval sense of humanity's closeness to eternity had clearly faded by the early 1600s, and a new note of urgency had sounded. Time had begun to accelerate, and the modern sense of time had been born.

In the sixteenth and seventeenth centuries, great centers of clock making arose in Augsburg, Nuremburg, Blois, Paris, and Lyon. Geneva and London became the major centers in the seventeenth and eighteenth centuries. Eventually, great clock-making workshops were also established in the Hague, Stockholm, and Copenhagen. While clock-making technology had made an early start in Catholic Italy, the industry never developed there as it did in the Protestant north, and, not coincidentally, science, which had made great strides in Italy during the Renaissance, also took center stage in Protestant northern Europe during this same period.

The full-blown notion of the clockwork universe and all it represents were a product of the new sensibility that arose with the Reformation. The Catholic south of Europe remained somewhat rooted in the old medieval and Renaissance view of time that perceived the universe as essentially static. God was in his heaven above his nine orders of angels, the world was arrayed below in neat and immutable fashion, and time was simply a matter of waiting until the great trumpet blast blew and ended the world as we knew it. Chronology, in the Middle Ages, was less important than morality. True, the scholars of the Renaissance introduced the idea of progress, but when seeking models of perfection they still looked backward to a golden age.

The Reformation, however, placed a new emphasis on the future, a focus that encouraged people not to waste time in the present, for time was a limited quantity, fast diminishing. Instead of reacting to the shortness of time by grasping all the pleasures you could from this life, the Reformers, especially the Puritans, recommended serious work and plenty of it.

As early as 1552, the English Parliament attempted to limit the number of holidays to only twenty-seven days. This restriction would have meant that, counting Sundays, there would be only seventy-nine holidays in the year, considerably fewer than in the medieval calendar. The Puritans were opposed to holidays because, as the etymology of the word indicates, most of these holidays were at least nominally "holy days," dedicated to saints in the Catholic Church calendar. Since these days were not in the Bible, the Puritans argued, and since most of them were associated with the papist notion of saints, they should be done away with. The Puritans wanted to model the week on Scripture and feature only one day in seven without work year-round.

This flew in the face of medieval tradition, which boasted a mind-boggling array of feast and festival days. Most of these ancient festivals were based on the agricultural cycle of work, which made for seasonal leisure. A quick look at the church's liturgical year shows that most of the important feasts, from Advent to Easter, are packed between fall harvest and spring planting. Summer too had its important festival times, such as St. John's Eve, known as Midsummer Night's Eve. There were also market fairs, which would be days without work, and weeklong wakes, or parish festivals.

In fact, prior to Puritanism's upsurge, people seem to have regarded work as an imposition on the generally festive nature of life, to be performed no more than necessary to maintain one's life in reasonable comfort. Old records indicate that people abandoned work quite readily when any other opportunity offered itself. In a fascinating book on the subject, *A Social History of Leisure Since 1600*, Gary Cross points out that preindustrial workers opted to play rather than accumulate more money. When costs of living decreased or when workers made more money for their products than usual, they responded not by producing more goods to make even more profit but by taking more leisure time. Workers often took off an additional weekly holy day known widely as St. Monday, an extension of the Sabbath made possible by leftover money from Saturday's pay and by the fact that materials did not arrive at shops until late Monday mornings or in the afternoon.

Naturally, the mostly middle-class and urban Puritans found this threatening. For merchant men and shop owners, time was money. From the Puritan point of view, regular work, especially if it was hard, was a method of improving humanity and rescuing it from depravity. In exchange for hard work, they believed, they would receive benefits here in the form of wealth and in the next world as well. Pleasure and enjoyment were postponed. "God sent you not into this world as into a Play-house, but a Work-house," as one early New Englander wrote.[13] The world of time was to be given over to self-improvement. As Increase Mather put it, "Every man's Eternity . . . will be according to his improvement of time here."[14] Leisure time, as it existed in the Middle Ages and in Catholic countries like France, Spain and Italy, was seen by the Puritans as little more than an occasion to sin and a threat to godliness.

John Calvin's *Institutes of the Christian Religion* called for the sanctification of the whole world, and as part of the purification there would be only one holiday, or holy day, per week. And that day would not be spent in such frivolous, if traditional, enjoyments as those available at the alehouse, the playhouse, and the cockpit. Time was not to be wasted on the Sabbath any more than it was during the week. The labor to be performed on Sunday was soul work. If any reading was done, it was to be the Bible, and if any singing, psalms alone were allowed. In Puritan New England, work was prohibited on Sunday, but so were travel and play and taking pleasure in life. In some places strolling might be tolerated, as long as you didn't let on you were enjoying it, and every English major is familiar with Massachusetts Colony sermons about boys who drowned on the Sabbath because they had indulged their pagan lust to swim instead of going to church to pray. Richard Baxter, in *A Christian Directory* (1673) wrote, "Remember still that the Time of this short uncertain life is all that ever you should have, for your preparation for your endless life. When this is spent, whether well or ill, you shall have no more."[15]

In the end, those who organized their lives by this new time consciousness seemed to prosper in ways others did not, and a new work climate was imposed by the now powerful owners of shops and factories. As the economy changed from an agricultural base to one based on trade and manufacture and eventually to industry, a major cultural trade-off was made: time for money. People exchanged personal and festive time for economic gain, and in the end time and money, even life itself, became equated. Even as non-Puritan a character as Ben Franklin could write in *Poor Richard's Almanac*, "Dost thou love life? Then do not squander Time, for that's the stuff Life is made of."

It was not the Puritans alone, however, who changed our notion of time. It was also profoundly changed by the emergence of the scientific way of looking at the world, for the clock, in many ways, is at the heart of science. Experiments and precise observations depend on predictability, regularity, and patterns measured over time, and the more precisely you can measure time, the more precise your calculations and therefore your grasp of reality will be.

Through the 1600s, the metaphor of the clockwork universe triumphed over older models of the world. The adoption of this concept seems to have been quite conscious and deliberate. Johannes Kepler (1571–1630) wrote, "My aim is to show that the celestial machine is to be likened not to a divine organism but rather to a clockwork."[16] Robert Boyle (1627–1691), writing of the universe, said, "it is like a rare clock, such as may be that at Strasbourg, where all things are so skillfully contrived, that the engine being once set a-moving, all things proceed according to the artificer's first design, and the motions . . . do not require the particular interposing of the artificer, or any intelligent agent employed by him, but perform their functions upon particular occasions, by virtue of the general and primitive contrivance of the whole engine."[17]

Through the seventeenth century, clocks gained in accuracy and precision. The Dutchman Christian Huygens (1629–1695) developed the pendulum regulator, which increased the accuracy of clocks by a factor of nearly one hundred, reducing daily error in clocks from about one thousand seconds a day to only ten. It would be another century before a similar increase in accuracy was achieved. Huygens also wrote a philosophical treatise called *Traité de la lumière*, in which he claimed that the universe ran on mechanical principles alone, like a great clock.

In light of the great technical achievements in clock making and the social changes involved in the standardization of time, it is no surprise that this period of history, 1600–1900, also saw a revolution in the conception of time itself. Time came to be regarded as a process that, like the clockwork universe, ticked on relentlessly regardless of our human, subjective experience of it. This was the notion of absolute time, born at the same time as the clockwork universe, and it led to an entirely new notion of history and of humanity's place in the stream of time.

Absolute time, like the seafaring clock and the notion of the clockwork universe, was an invention of the Age of Reason. In order for his celestial mechanics to work, Isaac Newton needed to think of time as a regular and measurable process, something that moved in one direction only and at a steady pace. Eventually, the notion of absolute time, which worked admirably well in physics, crept into general Western consciousness. Time now had the look of something absolute and steady. It soon lost its fluid, variable, and qualitative nature and became a regular, linear, and ongoing process progressing at a steady rate that was measurable by the eighteenth century's marvelous clocks. The universe became a clockwork through and through. It became more important than ever, over the next two hundred years, to know what time it was, for without that knowledge one would be out of sync not only with one's fellow beings but with the universe itself.

In society at large, clocks grew more popular as they grew small enough to enter the homes of the newly rich bourgeoisie, and, in the palaces of the nobles, clocks in highly gilded and ornamented cases became fixtures of baroque decor. Not everyone enjoyed having so many clocks around. A Madame Lovigny was said to have fled her Paris residence because the sound of so many chiming clocks from the nearby Hostel d'Epernon was cutting her life into too many little pieces.[18] French philosopher Jean-Jacques Rousseau (1712–1778) was said to have thrown his watch away in a Romantic gesture toward eternal time. But, by and large, clocks and clock time became woven into the fabric of European life during these centuries, and soon the image of the clockwork universe also became the dominant view of how the world was really put together. The embodiment of the whole conception was the orrery, named after its inventor, Charles Boyle (d. 1721), fourth earl of Orrery. It was a clockwork mechanism that used balls to represent the relative positions and motions of planets and other bodies in the solar system as they revolved around the sun. Turn the crank and the universe moved—like a clock!

As clocks grew more precise and as more people regulated their lives by them, a new notion of time began to emerge as well. The new, improved clocks of the seventeenth century "could tick away uniformly and continually for years on end, and so must have greatly strengthened belief in the homogeneity and continuity of time. The mechanical clock was therefore not only the prototype instrument for the mechanical conception of this universe but for the modern idea of time."[19] When people conceive of time flowing, as in a clepsydra or an hourglass, or when they live their lives by the path of the sun overhead, they tend to think of time as a

fluid, even malleable thing, having a rhythm that is sometimes quick and staccato, sometimes slow and languid, but
they probably don't experience it as Madame Lovigny did,
cutting their lives into little pieces. Once the clock took over
the European experience of time, however, and people began
to conform their lives to it, they stepped away from more
natural and organic metaphors of time and began to think of
it as an ever-moving process, never changing, never varying.
A minute was sixty seconds, never more, never less, and the
clock proved it. Once the metaphor of the clock got applied
to the workings of the universe, and once people used the
clock to link their lives to that mechanical universe, the
complex was complete. People attempted to live their lives
with the same sort of consistency and uniformity they expected from their clocks.

By the 1700s, clocks and pocket watches had become
nearly ubiquitous among the new bourgeoisie. In the late
eighteenth century, London watchmakers exported 80,000
timepieces of various kinds and produced another 50,000 for
domestic use. The clock makers of Geneva produced some
70,000 to 80,000 devices during the same time period.
Through seventeenth-century missionaries and eighteenth-
century traders, European clocks and European conceptions
of time were being introduced into lands as far away as
Turkey, China, and North America, and thus began the
worldwide movement to clock time and a clockwork universe.[20] According to Mumford, the fabric of daily life
changed as a result. The newly clocked middle classes "reduced life to a careful, uninterrupted routine: so long for
business: so long for dinner: so long for pleasure—all carefully measured out."[21] This mania for precision and living
life like clockwork reached its satiric height in the opening

chapters of Laurence Sterne's *Tristram Shandy*, in which Tristram's father's mania for winding his clock and having sex on the same Sunday each month allowed the hero to fix exactly the moment of his conception.

In a way, living life according to the clock was turning people into regular machines, just like music-playing automatons, those other marvelous mechanical products of the eighteenth-century clock age. So much did clock time come to rule people's everyday lives that it became important to know what time it was even at night. In order to avoid the trouble of lighting a candle in the dark, a Frenchman named Monsieur De Villayer designed a spice clock that had various spices inserted in holes in the face of the clock where the numbers were. Waking in the middle of the night, he could reach out, take a bit of spice from the hole nearest the hour hand, taste that it was cinnamon, and know that it was three o'clock in the morning.[22] This savory method never caught on. The problem of telling time in the dark was eventually solved with the invention of the repeater watch, which simply chimed the hour when a button was pushed.

The importance of clocks and precise timekeeping to the modern age resulted in an intense and fervid competition to produce ever more exact and reliable timepieces. Especially necessary to the world of science, exploration, and trade was the invention of a reliable seagoing clock, and the development of the marine chronometer may serve as a model for how a single invention can have enormous philosophical and social consequences.

The sixteenth and seventeenth centuries were great ages of European expansion into other parts of the world. Beginning with the Portuguese excursions down the coast of Africa as they inched their way toward the riches of India, the nations of Europe set out on a several-hundred-year project of extending their trade routes, and eventually their political domination, into virtually every corner of the earth.

In order to determine longitude and the precise ascension of stars, both navigators and astronomers needed precise clocks. The problem stems from the fact that sailors cannot know exactly where they are at sea without also knowing what time it is. They can tell their latitude by measuring the angle between the horizon and the sun when the shadow of a sundial shows noon and thus know their distance from the equator. But knowing their longitude depends on knowing where certain stars should be at specific times. The stars, except for the North Star, are in constant motion, and where they appear in the sky depends on when exactly they are seen. On land, a weight-driven clock or pendulum clock would work well enough for this, but those kinds of clocks are worthless on a pitching and rolling ship. Spring-driven clocks had been around in some form from about 1410, but no one had successfully addressed the fact that wound springs lose force as they unwind, and for a clock to tell time accurately an even force must be applied, like that provided by gravity in weight-driven clocks. A seafaring clock would also have to withstand wide variations in heat and cold, not to mention the problems caused by damp. Expansion and rust of metal parts were only minor complications, however, compared to the difficulty of devising a mechanism that would reliably and regularly move the gears to keep time accurate to within a few minutes over a months- or years-long voyage.

The financial consequences for the emerging commercial empires of Europe were enormous, and so a tremendous amount of time and creative energy went into schemes to make practical seafaring clocks. In the seventeenth and eighteenth centuries, Philip II of Spain, Louis XIV of France, and the States General of the Netherlands offered large cash prizes to anyone who could devise a machine to help sailors easily find their longitude. The British Parliament, under Queen Anne, offered an enormous prize of £20,000 (well over $1 million today) for a device that could successfully enable a ship to travel to the West Indies and back with an error of less than thirty minutes of longitude or two minutes of time.[23]

The prize, or most of it anyway, went to Englishman John Harrison, who, with his brother James, succeeded in creating a seagoing clock that on a voyage of some 4,500 miles brought the ship accurately to its destination.[24] Harrison's invention made time truly portable for the first time in history, which in turn made a reliable "standard time" possible, even inevitable.

Creating a standard time had never been a problem in the days before worldwide exploration. Local sun time was precise enough, and travel was so slow that a deviation of a few minutes from solar time would not make any difference. But if each community used its own solar time as its local time, then there could be a variation in time of nearly twenty minutes in less than two hundred miles. As systems like the post and intercity coach service developed in the 1700s, the need soon arose for a common time to make scheduling more convenient. The Royal Observatory at Greenwich, England, was ready to supply a way to develop a standard time.

The observatory, founded in 1675 under the reign of the science-minded Charles II (he also founded the Royal Society in 1660), established a prime meridian that arbitrarily, if somewhat egocentrically, set its own building at zero degrees longitude and its own time as the standard against which the various ships' clocks of the expanding British naval and commercial empire would tell time. Using the sundial, sailors would gauge their ships' clocks at the "apparent noon" at their own location and compare it to what eventually became known to navigators around the world as Greenwich mean time. Navigators from other nations eventually adopted the standard, thanks largely to *The Nautical Almanac*, which Greenwich began producing in 1767. This extremely accurate guide to star locations and geographic positions established Greenwich as the baseline for time calculations worldwide.

At first, the convenience of a standard time was for sailors only, since only sailors had to know the time that precisely. But soon other branches of society began to adopt standard time. The need for punctuality was increasingly felt by coach travelers, who were disconcerted by the twenty-minute difference between Bristol time and London time and similar time discrepancies that had never bothered anyone much before. The introduction of the faster-moving railroads in the early and mid-nineteenth century exacerbated the problem. On railway journeys, passengers had to reset their watches by a couple of minutes every few miles. Without standard time, schedules were impossible to regulate, and general confusion was widespread. In the United States and Canada, where the railroads spanned huge distances, the need for standard time was especially acute. In 1875, railroads in the United States imposed an *ad hoc* standard time. And in 1884, following a plan laid down a few years earlier by Canadian railway planner Sir Sandford Fleming, an international delegation representing twenty-seven nations met in Washington, D.C., and divided the earth into twenty-four time zones, each about fifteen degrees of longitude wide, using Greenwich as zero degrees. Time would be uniform within each zone. Hours would be different from zone to zone, but minutes and seconds would be standard so when it was 9:42:35 in New York, it was 8:42:35 in Chicago, 7:42:35 in Denver, 6:42:35 in San Francisco, and so on. (Today, only a few exceptions exist, like Newfoundland in Canada, which is one half hour different from the next time zone.)

It was thus possible for the entire world to ignore sun time and become monochronic, using a time-telling system that was becoming increasingly abstract and cut off from natural cycles, just as what constituted a "day's work" at a factory had been cut off from the cycle of sunrise and sunset. Railway time became the model for all time. Dickens, in *Dombey and Son*, after several sentences on the ubiquity of railroads in mid-century England, wrote, "There was even railway time observed in clocks, as if the sun itself had given in."[25] And in *Walden* Henry David Thoreau wrote,

I watch the passage of the morning cars with the same feeling that I do the rising of the sun, which is hardly more regular . . . The startings and arrivals of the cars are now the epochs in the village day. They go and come with such regularity and precision and their whistle can be heard so far, that the farmers set their clocks by them, and thus one well-conducted institution regulates a whole country. Have not men improved somewhat in punctuality since the railroad was invented? Do they not talk and think faster in the depot than they did in the stage office?[26]

After World War I, this railroad time became everyone's time as common people began to wear watches for the first time. Soldiers got in the habit during the war because watches were needed to synchronize troop movements and attacks. As modern mass society emerged after the war, the battle model was kept: civilians too would become synchronized. Twentieth-century business, industry, and society, extending the Industrial Revolution into every aspect of life, called for an intricate social organization all based on the clock. In fact, Lewis Mumford, in his 1934 classic *Technics and Civilization*, identified the clock as the underpinning of modern civilization. "The first characteristic of modern machine civilization is its temporal regularity," wrote Mumford, giving the clock status as the archetypal machine of the machine age.[27] As Mumford pointed out, our era saw the final absorption of personal time by public time. Now virtually every aspect of life runs "by the clock." We time our eating by it; we time our work by it. Many people even worry about how many minutes intimate events like sexual intercourse "ought" to take.

Today, cesium atomic clocks, which set the standard for precision, are accurate to within 0.0000001 seconds per day, an incredible advance over the first medieval clocks, which could lose or gain as much as 1,000 seconds per day and often had to be reset against sundials, which were more accurate. The atomic clock utilizes a beam of cesium atoms passed across a vacuum, during which the atoms emit photons at a steady frequency that is measured to determine the exact passage of time.[28] A second, measured this way, is exactly 1/31,556,925.9747 of a solar year. Unlike the steady flow of a water clock or the regular tick of the mechanical clock, or even the piezoelectric hum of a quartz watch, these atomic clocks make no noise. They do not flow, or tick or hum; they wink. They are also unbelievably accurate. Measuring time this precisely is a highly specialized occupation. Only a few hundred people around the world can do it. Each time we call the time service to set our watches, the ultimate reference is the atomic clock. We strap this precise time to our wrist and proceed with our day, coordinating our personal time to this absolute time, which seems separate from us, given to us by nature itself. It winks on, regardless of all, in a steady progression.

By the mid-twentieth century, the secularization of time was nearly complete. Absolute time, more precise clocks, and the worldwide standardization of time had effectively divorced time from our subjective experience of it. Time marched on with or without us, out of an infinite past and into an infinite future, and our own lives seemed pitifully short in comparison. Like a great machine, time continued to run mindlessly and pointlessly onward, accelerating as the century progressed. We now know, with a precision never dreamed of before, just what time it is, but what we gained in mathematical precision we lost in a sense of connection to eternity. Ever-moving time is now more and more a thing to be saved rather than savored. The more we can frantically squeeze into it the better, for our time here is all too brief in the vast flow of things. The only good news is that, with precise chronometers, we can measure our finitude and mortality with greater and greater accuracy, but the point of it all seems lost somehow.

As we've seen, the changes in Western culture's sense of time occurred very gradually, over several hundred years. As a result, we who are born into the modern sense of time do not even notice anything odd about it. The historic change was like the acceleration of the Japanese bullet train that glides out of the station so smoothly that you don't notice how soon you are traveling nearly 200 miles per hour. Like the *shinkansen*, our acclerated culture is now hurtling down its tracks carrying us along more swiftly than we may care to go, and it resists our best efforts to slow it down. Indeed, we have so internalized the rhythm that when we stop, we often greet our leisure time (time when we are not obligated to do anything) as a dreary void. Instead of welcoming it as the fullness of time, we may sense a frightening vacuum.

Perhaps the metaphor of time famine is not quite accurate. We are perhaps crammed with time, but with the wrong kind. Like people who eat too much junk food, we have filled our lives with the wrong kind of time, and rarely if ever do we avail ourselves of the kind of time that will truly nourish our spirits.

The search for sacred time may begin as a simple search for rest and refreshment. In fact, as we'll see, real sacred time might lie along a continuum that begins with simply kicking back or ceasing our daily work, and then ends in the deepest raptures of mystical union with the godhead. In a world dominated by the clock, we spend every waking moment filling the minutes and hours that come at us, never resting, never feeling we have "enough" time. Just as we accumulate material possessions yet never feel we have enough, so we feel a lack of time. We long for a period when we can say, "I am satisfied," and can repose in the sense of fullness that follows. The ancient notion of the fullness of time has eroded, replaced by a constant sense of want and need.

"In the fullness of time" is a beautiful biblical expression. It means a miraculous moment in which the eternal and the temporal meet. But more, fullness suggests that far from experiencing time as a void, we can experience it as an abundance. From moment to moment, time does not deliver us empty bottles to be filled, but instead it offers us the very fecundity, the prolific life-giving quality, of the universe itself. The source of life that creates and sustains the whole universe, that drives the life of plants and upholds all creation, also flows through us. When we can tap into that source, become aware of it coursing through our veins as it does all the time, then we may say, "It is enough."

But the ability to access the fullness of time lies along the vertical axis of our being, in the experience of what we call the eternal or the divine. The triumph of the clock, whose march toward victory we have just briefly traced, prevents us from experiencing time's abundance. It has convinced us that attempts to slow down what we call progress, or to put our daily lives on hold for even brief periods, is a terrible waste of time.

All is not hopeless, however. Like a seed in dry ground, the ability to experience the fullness of time exists in us as a potential, capable of being quickened back to life. But, like a newly sprung plant, the sense of sacred time also needs care and nurturing if it is to bloom and flourish.

Fortunately, the sacred traditions of the world provide us with a multitude of proven ways of experiencing sacred time. In the now nearly forgotten practice of the Sabbath, for example, we may find a pathway to the meaning of sacred time. Experiencing the fullness of time, as we'll see, is still possible even in our fast-paced, time-starved world. There may not be much we have to do in order to experience it, but first we may have to learn a whole new way to be.

CHAPTER 6

In Search of Sacred Time

WESTERN AND WESTERNIZED CULTURES are thoroughly dominated by clock time. In other places, however, every day is lived out with frequent excursions into sacred time. Friends of mine who visited Ghana told me about the reaction they got when they asked if they would have a chance to see some ritual dancing or drumming. Of course, they were told. Everyday life is a constant dance. Each day the drums beat for something. In such a culture, the sacred and profane are never far apart. When I was in Japan, my hosts would place a bit of the day's rice in a bowl in the family shrine and leave it there to consecrate it. In that busy industrialized country, this ritual seemed a relic of an earlier time, yet I saw it frequently. In Islamic societies, believers still bow to Mecca and pray five times a day.

In our own culture, it seems that only remnants of this ritual ambience remain. Once in a while one can hear the Angelus bell ring above downtown traffic, but most of our days begin with no thought of the sacred at all. We regard morning prayers or ablutions as superstitions. Instead, we ritually listen to the news, catching up with what is happening in the hectic world of time. Eternity? Who has time for it? Anyway, by definition it's always there, so we can get to it later.

This secular attitude had its origins in the Enlightenment. First and foremost about the triumph of reason, the Enlightenment also marked the beginning of the end of the Age of Faith in the West. After a century of bloody wars fought by Christians over fine theological distinctions, Enlightenment philosophers may be excused for seeing religion as an impediment to human progress. And clearly the Enlightenment, or the *Erklärung*, as the Germans call it, did clarify much. Within the first hundred years or so of the Age of Reason, incredible advances were made in the human understanding of the physical world in such areas as medicine, astronomy, chemistry, and physics. As a result, however, the gulf between the religious and the scientific worldviews widened. By the mid-1800s, thinking people had to decide between religion and science. Charles Darwin, Karl Marx, and others had pointed out too many inconsistencies and shortcomings of the religious worldview. The new criticism in scriptural studies cast doubts on the reliability of Scripture. The net result was that by the close of the nineteenth century most progressive minds were firmly on the side of science. Forward-thinking individuals were aware a serious problem was created by separating what they believed from what they knew, but they seemed incapable of resolving it, for the religious and the scientific worldviews seemed diametrically opposed.

The mechanistic, deterministic worldview triumphed fully in the twentieth century. Most people, certainly most in the United States, now subscribe more to a scientific worldview than a religious one. Of course, most Americans, in polls, will say they believe in God. But professing to a pollster you believe in a higher power and organizing your life that way are two different things. In fact, based on the way most people live today, it seems clear that we live in a demythologized

world in which secular materialism has, for the time, overcome almost all vestiges of mythology and religion. So, not
surprisingly, we have lost a sense of what sacred time is and
could be.

Around the turn of the twentieth century, European and
American sociologists and anthropologists set out to study
"primitive" peoples. Coming in as outsiders to cultures that
they often regarded as inferior to their own, they set about
systematically cataloging mythologies, folkways, and social
patterns, and in the process they revealed much about their
own belief (or nonbelief) systems. The pioneers in these fields
came from a European intellectual tradition already well into
a process of secularization prone to divide the world into du-
alities like civilized and uncivilized, modern and primitive,
and sacred and profane. Coming out of the Enlightenment
tradition, they often regarded the world they observed as the
result of the interplay of merely material forces and often set
up diametric oppositions where today we might see more
fluid processes. Religion and religious experience became
identified with such pejorative adjectives as primitive, uncivilized, and backward.

This should not be too surprising. In *Theories of Primitive Religion*, British anthropologist E. E. Evans-Pritchard
observes that the nineteenth- and twentieth-century writers
who were most influential in forming modern ideas of religion (he includes Edward Burnett Tylor, James George
Frazer, Bronislaw Malinowski, Emil Durkheim, Lucien Lévy-
Bruhl, and Sigmund Freud) were, when they wrote their
works, either agnostics or atheists. Implied in their point of
view were certain Enlightenment assumptions about religion that were inherited from eighteenth-century rationalist
philosophers. To many of them, as to Marx, religion was a

drug used by the ruling classes to keep the common classes ignorant, lazy, and superstitious so they could be "exploited in the name of religion by cunning and avaricious priests and the unscrupulous classes which supported them."[1] The world of science, represented by the social scientists, and the world of religion were seen as separate realms and opposing ways of thought. Of the sacred realm and the profane, Durkheim wrote, "In all the history of human thought there exists no other example of two categories of things so profoundly differentiated or so radically opposed to one another. . . . The sacred and the profane have always and everywhere been conceived by the human mind as two distinct classes, as two worlds between which there is nothing in common."[2] Religious phenomena, he continues, "always suppose a bipartite division of the whole universe, known and knowable, into two classes which embrace all that exists, but which radically exclude each other."[3]

This radical separation of the sacred and the profane seems today to be a product of Durkheim's rationalism, which tends to see things in absolute terms and in opposition. It could even be seen as a modernist relic. It remains, however, very much the way we see things, and perhaps we can use it as a starting point in our search to fully understand what we mean by sacred time.

Rather than thinking of the sacred and profane as absolute opposites, we can think of them as shifting gestalts, two different lenses through which we can view the experience of life. The metaphor is of a pair of odd binoculars with one tube focused on things far off and the other on things nearby. Trying to look through both lenses at once blurs the view, but closing one eye and looking through the other allows us to see clearly. Regarded through the lens of profane time, the material world looks like a sequence of unrepeatable events, a combination of physical processes and material forces. Looked at through the lens of sacred time, however, the physical world is seen as something of an illusion permeated by the far more real world of spirit that exists outside the normal laws of time and space and unifies all things.

The modernist dilemma, following the Enlightenment, was that we felt we had to choose either one way of looking at things or the other, because only one way could be true. This division of the sacred from the profane worldview ignored the possibility of a third way of experiencing the world, namely, through ritual, which puts us in a threshold state where we experience things as both here and not here, now and not now.[4] This state is illogical and defies reason, but it nonetheless can be experienced. Victor Turner in *The Ritual Process* and Mircea Eliade in his many works have explored this territory quite well, but in our search for sacred time it would be good to review their work. Essentially, the ritual occurs in a threshold between the world we call sacred and the world we call profane. A person who stands exactly on the threshold between a hallway and a room is neither in nor out of either place. A step forward moves the person into the room, a step backward into the hallway, but on the threshold itself he or she is in an intermediate place that is simultaneously part of both places. The purpose of rituals, of trying to experience sacred time, is to allow us to psychologically inhabit the liminal or threshold area where the conventional distinction between sacred and profane is experienced as false and we can see through both lenses at once. In the liminal state of ritual time, one understands that the sacred and the profane are equally present always, only our day-to-day lens does not allow us to realize this.

An analysis of a typical ritual structure, following Turner and Eliade, will show us how religious ritual allows us to step outside the normal flow of what we call profane time and to experience and draw nourishment from what we call sacred time. To enter sacred time and space, we must first separate it ritually from profane space and time. The ritual space can be as simple as a circle drawn in the dirt by a magician or as architecturally complex as a cathedral or a ziggurat. Such a division of space has the effect of separating off a territory that, through a rite of purification or dedication, becomes isolated from the profane world, yet still connected to it.

The typical sacred space—a Japanese temple complex or a European cathedral—will have some sort of impressive threshold that must be crossed or passed through. The *torii*, or arch, in Japan forms such a gateway, as do the massive doors of a cathedral. In modern church architecture, a narthex or large doors are typically used to mark off the sacred precinct. The Latin word *templum*, from which we derive the English word temple, meant a place marked out for reading auguries or performing rites. Plato in his *Laws* referred to a religious holiday as *anapaula*, a "breathing space," suggesting that removing oneself from ordinary space and time allows the soul to breathe, to expand, to grow.[5]

But we must avoid carrying bits of the time-bound world with us into the sacred space, so most rituals begin with some sort of cleansing to rid ourselves of the impurities of the ordinary world. People entering Zen temples and Islamic mosques take off their shoes to keep out the literal dirt of the world and to remind them that they are walking on holy ground, with nothing separating them from it. At fountains outside Zen temples and mosques, pilgrims may also wash their hands and feet. In Catholic churches, a vestige of ritual cleansing still exists in the holy water font with which believers bless themselves on entering. By these and other ritual gestures, we remind ourselves that we are about to cross a threshold as psychological as it is physical. If the rite is efficacious, the believer begins at this point to shift out of the gestalt with which he or she faces the everyday world and turns toward the gestalt of eternity. Clock time should, ideally, cease to matter here.

The rite of entry is signified in a vast number of ways, well documented by anthropologists. A song, a drumbeat, a dance, a peal of bells, the donning of special vestments or masks, the recitation of formulas like "The Lord be with you," the burning of incense all serve to shift our consciousness into the realm of the sacred and have the potential to transport us into the liminal realm Turner describes so well.

According to Eliade, ritual "interrupts" the flow of profane time, as though we step outside of time, but it might be clearer to say that in the threshold time of ritual, the rite itself reveals the true nature of time. The ritual experience shows us profane time as something of an illusion concealing sacred time, which exists as a substrate to all we experience. Entering the ritual space allows us to see the correct relationship between time and eternity, which is that beneath the hurried rhythm of everyday life there is a slower, eternal rhythm. In the world of profane time, things happen once and for all, but in the world of sacred time, anything is possible; time may be reversed, identities may be transformed. Where the world of normal time is rigid, the world of sacred time is fluid.

Thus, once we have passed beyond the rite of entry and are in the liminal state, we may hold efficacious rituals. The archetypal rites are those of transformation or rites of passage. A boy enters his *bar mitzvah* ceremony and, a little over an hour later, he emerges as a man. A convert undergoes baptism and, through the working of the water, becomes a member of a community to which she was a mere aspirant only shortly before. Rites for the dead enable the souls of those once alive to pass over into death, and they provide a vehicle through which survivors can negotiate their grief. In a wedding, a single man and a single woman become husband and wife. They can be changed so profoundly because the threshold nature of ritual time brings us to a place where the usual categories we use to understand the world are dissolved.

Human ingenuity has devised nearly infinite variations on how rituals are organized, but beneath the brilliant panoply of rites making up the world's spiritual traditions, there seems to be a common pattern: we must leave profane time and space and enter the zone of the sacred in order to effect significant changes in ourselves.

In addition to rites of transformation, there are also rites of intensification, like the Christian Eucharist, which do not effect changes but intensify a belief already held. Participating in them allows the believer to recharge his or her faith by experiencing in sacred time the underlying reality of union with others that communion represents. Similarly, the rituals of the Jewish Sabbath each week intensify the sacred beliefs and experiences of the Jews.

Throughout the year, festivals and feast days allow us to reenter certain privileged times when, myths tell us, the gods consorted with human beings and the true nature of things was revealed. By entering the threshold state of ritual, where linear time is abolished, we become contemporaries of the mythological characters and move, for a time, in sync with the rhythms of their existence.

Finally, when the main rite of transformation or intensification is over, we must return to our day-to-day lives. A rite of exit is necessary. The sacred fires must be extinguished, the incense put out. Vestments must be taken off. "Go in peace, the mass is ended" is the Catholic formula. Bowing and exiting backward is common in Zen temples.

Outside the sacred precinct, "normal" life returns, but we feel changed, refreshed. Joseph Campbell said that when we emerge from an effective ritual, we come out with a sense that the world as we find it is "just so," the way it ought to be. That is the meaning of Amen: so be it. The ritual time ends in affirmation. After Sabbath, we begin our week again, reassured, at peace with ourselves and our world.

A brilliant analysis of how our culture has disengaged from sacred time was given some years ago by the Catholic philosopher Josef Pieper in several books dealing with work, leisure, celebration, and ritual. In analyzing the two great economic models of the twentieth century, capitalism and communism, Pieper saw some striking similarities in their attitudes toward work and life, attitudes that made entry into true sacred time virtually impossible.

He begins with the medieval philosophers' distinction between the *artes serviles*, or useful arts, and the ars liberalis, or liberal arts. The *artes serviles* procure us food, clothing, and shelter. They provide immediate goods and services and achieve some clearly defined goals. Most of the work we do in connection with our jobs or with household maintenance (cutting the grass, fixing the plumbing) belongs to this category.

The *ars liberalis*, on the other hand, refer to "work that does not have a purpose outside itself, that is meaningful in itself, and for that very reason is neither useful in the strict sense, nor servile, nor serviceable."[6] This is not to say that no work is involved in these liberal arts. On the contrary, people may sink tremendous time, money, and energy into them. The community resources marshaled for a large civic or religious ritual, for example, may involve more "work" than producing the basic commodities needed for food, clothing, and shelter. People may even do without in order to bring a sacred festival to life. To stage a carnival or to produce an elaborate ritual like a wedding may take more effort than tilling a field or running a small corporation. The essential difference is not in the amount of work performed but in the intention and purpose of the work.

In the twentieth century, the communists were often criticized for reducing everyone's worth to their economic value as workers. In the totalitarian states of Eastern Europe, the rhetoric of the proletariat encouraged people to think of themselves first and foremost as members of a production collective, of value to society only insofar as they could contribute to the production of goods and services. The result was the dull, drab, colorless life we glimpsed fitfully through gaps in the old Iron Curtain, a life lived in multistory living blocks inhabited by people who wore gray, ill-fitting clothing.

In the West, meanwhile, we prided ourselves on our lifestyle, by which we primarily meant a higher grade of plumbing and brighter fashions, proof that what we called "the American way of life" was superior to life in the various socialist republics. We had commodities galore, and we wallowed in our material abundance. And yet, as Pieper was perceptive enough to notice, another kind of totalitarianism was creeping into the industrialized Western world: the totalitarianism of work. He did not mean to imply that there were no differences between the world formed by capitalism and that produced by communism, but one thing they did seem to have in common was that in both worlds people were

increasingly defined by the work they did. The typical conversation opener in our world is "What do you do?" by which
we mean "What is your job?" A person in our society who
does not have a "job" feels apologetic and does a great deal of
explaining just why he or she is not "working." The question
"What do you do?" could have any number of answers. I garden. I read mysteries. I play the xylophone. But the one really
acceptable answer in our culture is to state the job for which
we are paid a wage.

The totalitarianism of work assumes that a person is what
he or she does for a living and that no sphere of a person's life
exists outside of that. Extreme examples come from the
"corporate man" era of the 1950s, when some companies
explicitly told upper-level executives which clubs they could
belong to, which levels of fellow employees they could associate with, and what were the acceptable boundaries of corporate dress. All aspects of one's life, including the suburb one
lived in, were more or less overtly controlled by the corporation, either through outright policy or powerful peer pressure.

The situation today is only superficially better. While
most corporations are probably enlightened enough not to
put specific limits on their employees' private lives, there is
perhaps more sense than ever that one is what one does. Most
obviously it is seen in the disappearance of true leisure, as
documented in Juliet Schor's 1991 book *The Overworked American*. Though some of her data have been challenged in recent
years, there is little question that most Americans today feel
they have less free time than ever, whether or not outside ob-
servers can measure this erosion objectively. The emergence of
the dual-income household has drastically reduced the
amount of time a family has available for nonwork activities.
The result, Pieper would say, is that we have forgotten what

true leisure is. The final triumph of the Protestant work ethic may be not just that we have forgotten how to pray but that we have even forgotten how to play. And play, a certain sense of "as if," is vital to experiencing sacred time.

Leisure and play, in Pieper's sense, are not what most modern people engage in during those brief times when they are not working. The most common leisure activity named by Americans in polls is watching television, an impoverished use of one's free time by Pieper's definition. When not watching television, many people actually pride themselves in "working at" their play. Whether it is golf, jogging, or tennis, these activities that were once primarily games and pastimes have become challenges to be mastered. Instead of simply enjoying knocking a ball around, contemporary practitioners of leisure activities expect to progress in them until they achieve a level of performance as close as possible to that of highly paid professionals. What is lost, it seems, is a sense of simple pleasure not connected with some goal, in other words, a sense of fun. Perhaps, in spite of the amount of money we spend each year on sports equipment, we have somehow lost the ability to be playful.

All of this may seem a long way from the topic of keeping the Sabbath, but it isn't, for leisure, the arts, and a spirit of play are absolutely essential for religious experience. If we make a habit of turning every activity into goal-directed work, then whether we are on the job or on the jogging track we are practicing the *artes serviles* instead of the *ars liberalis*. Perhaps we are spiritually undernourished without being aware of it, just as a person raised on junk food may not even be able to conceive of any other kind of nourishment. The problem might lie in a failure of imagination. Never having known anything but work, we have an attenuated notion of leisure. As Pieper says, "to be tied to the process of work may be ultimately due to the inner impoverishment of the individual: in this context everyone whose life is completely filled by his work . . . is a proletarian because his life has shrunk inwardly, and contracted, with the result that he can no longer act significantly outside his work, and perhaps can no longer even conceive of such a thing."[7]

A brief exploration of modern leisure time, therefore, might be a good way to begin the attempt to rediscover just what sacred time is. Ironically, there is no real shortage of leisure time available to us, whatever we may feel. Many of us have two-day weekends. In addition, we have national and bank holidays, religious holidays, and days off work we label "personal time." The situation, in one sense anyway, is much better than it was during the early days of the Industrial Revolution and in some ways even better than in the preindustrial days of agricultural work. In other ways, however, there have been drastic changes in the notion of leisure time that have in turn eroded our sense of what sacred time is all about.

In a fascinating study of changes in the concept of leisure time since the Industrial Revolution, Hugh Cunningham pinpoints a significant shift in the relationship between work and leisure that took place during the nineteenth century as Britain, the United States, and other countries made the transition from agricultural to industrialized societies.

In preindustrial societies, the nature and pace of work was quite different from our experience of it. The typical workday, though often long, was not organized like our current workday. Tales abound of workers at, say, a blacksmith shop finishing a job and then taking a long break for a game of quoits or a pint of ale. Larking on the job consisted of more than merely the equivalent of trying to sneak in a game of computer solitaire. Cockfights, races, and other games punctuated the workday. For those whose work took place inside the home, such as cottage weavers, many opportunities would have existed for breaking from work and taking leisure at frequent intervals with one's family. In preindustrial society, the line between work and free time could have been very fluid.

The industrial system put an end to that type of rhythm. Machines could work continuously at the same pace without fatigue, and the essence of factory work as it evolved in the early 1800s was that both the machines and the hands that operated them repeated the same motions over and over in a machine-set pace. Tamara Hareven, in a study of an early New England factory town, notes that the workers experienced a new kind of pressure, that of being subject to regimented time schedules governed by the bell or whistle of the factory.[8] Monotony, repetition, and indoor work cut off from the cycles of the sun took their toll, and many workers left the factories as much because of their inability to adapt to the new time sense as from the noise, dirt, and danger. But the factory system and its new tempo of work eventually won out, of course, and with it came rapid urbanization and a new idea of entertainment, recreation, and the uses of leisure time.

Prior to the factory system, recreation consisted largely of free rural entertainments such as harvest homes, local church festivals, and other intermittent feasts. These were often sponsored by wealthy landowners in Britain or, in the more democratic United States, were community affairs, potlucks, to which each brought his or her contribution. Traditionally, there were huge numbers of festal days through the year. The ancient Romans had 175 public holidays per year. In the 1600s, even in Paris, there were some 103 official holidays per year. By contrast, in the contemporary United States, including the fifty-two Sundays of the year, we have about sixty such days. Most of the old holidays were expressions of communal life in precapitalist society, celebrations of spring planting, sheep shearing, harvest, and local saints. The early industrialist JosiahWedgwood, writing in 1776, complained about these agricultural holdovers. He bemoaned the fact that his workers had been "at play" for four days and he couldn't get them back to work. He promised them an extra-long Christmas break, but to no avail. They were simply having too much fun at their local parish festival to come back to the pottery factory.[9]

As the century progressed, however, leisure time got commodified. First of all, factory regimentation meant that recreation could take place only on weekends. Then, off-duty factory workers were given new, urbanized ways of "recreating" themselves, nearly all of them involving spending their money on entertainments that were frankly commercial in their intent. Music halls, penny arcades, and, after the coming of the railroads, commercial recreation parks like Blackpool in England and Coney Island in the United States gave workers a chance to spend some of their extra money to purchase an afternoon of entertainment.

Since then, the commercialization of recreation has become so entrenched that today we find it hard to imagine any other kind. Even as simple a thing as walking can seemingly require purchasing the proper shoes, outfit, hand weights, sweatbands, and personal sound system. There is nothing in itself wrong with that, of course. It's just that you get what you pay for: if all you're looking for is a mere "pastime" to divert yourself until you go back to work again, then paid-for recreation time is sufficient. But if mere diversion becomes a substitute for entering true sacred time, then it is like a junk food diet, not truly giving us the nourishment we need.

The quintessential example of the trend toward substituting commercial entertainment for deeper experiences of leisure might be Super Bowl Sunday. Sociologists point out that this day has become a national ritual. The sheer popularity of the event suggests that it reflects some deeply held American values. Yet, in the end, it remains a secular and materialistic ritual, not touching the heart and soul of true ritual. The Monday following Super Bowl Sunday usually comes without much sense of renewal or delight, even if your team has won.

Super Bowl Sunday is not the only secular ritual we celebrate. So strong is the trend toward celebrating materialism that many formerly religious holidays have also devolved into merely secular events more concerned with consuming things than celebrating life itself. Christmas, in many interesting ways, is now no different from Super Bowl Sunday, except that the hype lasts longer and more merchandise is sold. The vestiges of the true holy day are still there, but the soul seems gone. Gift giving, which should be an expression of the delight we take in life, has become the be-all and end-all of the modern American Christmas holiday. In a secular society, the thing itself, its size, its price, its "thingness" become the point. Each year, of course, dozens of movies remind us that Christmas is not about things, but the message of *It's a Wonderful Life* seems to get lost in the avalanche of commercials surrounding it.

But what of those other, more cerebral or cultural ways we spend our leisure time? What about Sunday afternoons at the art museum or the concert hall? What about reading a good book? These worthy activities certainly lie along the spectrum between mere diversion and a full experience of sacred time, but even they fall somewhat short of the mark.

The very idea of spending a Sunday afternoon in a museum is a fairly recent phenomenon. Like consumption-based recreation, it seems to date back only to the nineteenth century, when cultural institutions like public parks, libraries, and museums were established for the moral improvement of the working classes. The archetype in England was the Great Exhibition of 1851, held at the Crystal Palace in Hyde Park. The newly established railroads brought trainloads of people to London to gaze in wonder at the latest technological wonders the industrial age had brought to the world. Progress was on display, and the masses came by the millions to worship at its cathedral. It was part of a secular and religious movement called "rational recreation," whose goal was to move the cause of civilization forward by inculcating a taste for the fine arts, learning, and culture in the lower classes. To a large extent, it succeeded. Today, spending a Sunday afternoon visiting a museum, attending a public lecture, or listening to a concert of classical music is, for many people, a secular substitute for regular church going. Yet all of these self-improving activities still fall short as experiences of sacred time. Aesthetic rapture, as pleasant as it may be, is only the beginning of the experience of the fullness of time.

And what of church going? Is that, finally, where we will find sacred time? Not necessarily. When it comes to experiencing sacred time, going to church can be as secular as any other activity. If, as for many, church going is only one more duty to check off one's weekly list, or if it becomes yet another flurry of busyness, full of nothing but prepping lessons for Sunday school, baking cookies for the reception, and serving on committees, then it can become as much a source of feeling frustrated and frazzled as everything else in the modern world.

What then is sacred time? We are back to the idea of a gestalt shift. Experiencing sacred time is somewhat like looking at an optical illusion. If you look one way, the drawing of the cube appears to recede into the page; if you change your focus, it appears to come toward you. So too with shifting to a sacred view of the world. It seems that once people could move quite freely between the sacred and the profane views of things, but in the past hundred years or so we as a culture have become so determinedly secular that we may have lost the knack. In fact, even the distinction we make between secular and profane time may be a product of our modern secular way of thinking.

So what, then, in Pieper's terms, is sacred time? It "is essentially a phenomenon of wealth: not, to be sure, the wealth of money, but of existential richness."[10] What is celebrated in the religious festival or ritual is not all those things created by us in the world of work, but all those things that are simply given to us, beginning with the simple fact of our existence and extending to all of creation. And what is required of us in the festival is simply to enjoy. Nothing more, nothing less. "The trick," writes Pieper, "is not to arrange a festival, but to find people who can enjoy it."[11] This is the gestalt shift necessary to experience sacred time.

Perhaps the reason we have let ourselves grow so out of touch with sacred time is that it does not involve making profit or even making progress. In fact, it entails letting go of the things, like our sense of a lack of material goods or the desire to attain greater proficiency in one of our recreation activities, that normally drive our lives, and simply rejoicing in what we have.

Sheer enjoyment of life, pure celebration, however, involves a quality of play and playfulness, an act of the imagination, a capacity to act "as if" that our modern education and work-obsessed lifestyles have allowed to atrophy in us. We live in a society where non-goal-directed activity is actively discouraged. Children cannot simply dance; they must be in a dance program. Kids can't just play baseball; they must be in a competitive league. All of these activities, to be sure, carry some measure of pleasure, even a sense of accomplishment, but they may not be real leisure in Pieper's sense.

The first step toward finding sacred time, then, must be to rest completely from one's labors. But simply "not working" is not enough to experience the fullness of sacred time. If all one does is not work, then boredom quickly sets in, and ennui is already one of the hallmarks of our era. In this age of constant diversion and a profusion of leisure options, one of the chronic complaints, ironically, is of boredom. I constantly meet college students, at what should be the peak of their life's enthusiasm, who tell me they are bored. They act bored. Nothing seems to interest them. Gifted with all the riches and potential a materialistic society can give them, they nonetheless remain unengaged, unenthused. They call themselves slackers. It is as though they have not learned how to be excited about life itself. Like the rest of us, they surf through a hundred cable channels and complain, "There's nothing on." What they and we mean, of course, is that we have lost the ability to become engaged in anything our society offers us. Like people whose appetites have been sated, we have forgotten what it means to be hungry, and nothing tempts us. In spite of our frenetic activity, we live in an age of slacking. But this ennui is not a problem of the external world. Creation itself is not worn out. We are. "One can only be bored if the spiritual power to be leisurely has been lost."[12]

So, then, what is true leisure and what is its connection to the holy?

The Hebrew Scriptures suggest that cessation of labor is only a beginning, but it is a necessary first step, for stopping work carves out a portion of time the way drawing a circle on the ground marks out a portion of space. As the temple is an area set aside for sacred activities, taking a period for leisure sets aside a time during which we may contemplate. Contemplation requires time.

Once the time is marked out as a certain day or a certain hour during which we do not work, then what follows is the celebration. Feast days, Sabbaths, anniversary days, even half hours set aside for sitting on a meditation cushion are recognized as privileged points of time, having a special emotional coloring and intensity. They are times of signification, when we recognize that there is more to us, and to the world, than simply work. When we stop working, we develop "a receptive attitude of mind, a contemplative attitude," and we then open within us "the capacity for steeping [ourselves] in the whole of creation."[13]

Ancient writers understood the holy nature of leisure time that was devoted to contemplation, festival and celebration. Plato said that a festival occurred in *hieros chronos*, holy time, and in his *Laws* he noted that the muses, the sources of the creative arts, were given to humankind as companions for festivals, so that a life lived with attention to the *ars liberalis*, or those things not connected with our work selves, could potentially be festive 365 days a year. Pythagoras wrote that, properly understood, life itself is a *panegyris*, a festival.

Early Christians also seemed to have understood from the

start the festal nature of sacred time. Clement of Alexandria wrote, "We spend our whole lives like a feast day." Athanasius, in the fourth century, said that the celebration of the Eucharist represented to Christians an unobstructed passageway to the eternal realm and the timeless origin of all things. When one uses leisure to open a space in time for celebration, then the fullness of being rushes in. Chrysostom wrote, "We have unending holiday" and "Where love rejoices, there is festivity." Even the solitary and grave Jerome wrote, "ours . . . is an eternal festival." Augustine chimed in with, "In the house of God, festivity is perpetual." Aquinas, in his *Summa Theologica*, says that on festive days we celebrate the *beneficium creationis*, the gift of being created. For the Christian, the Sabbath or festal day of true leisure prefigures the end of time. It is the *imago venturi saeculi*, the image of the coming age, when we will move beyond this world of work and pain and will be immersed in pure being. Even the Enlightenment philosopher Rousseau understood the festive nature of life itself. "Put a flower-decked pole in the middle of an open place, call the people together—and you have a fête."[14]

The heart of leisure, and therefore of entering and celebrating sacred time, does not lie in "doing nothing." Doing nothing is what people in the Middle Ages called sloth, and they made a distinction between it and leisure. Sloth led to idleness and restlessness, what they called *acedia*, an irritability, a lack of calm and peace, the sort of boredom and sense of "nothing to do" that can lead in teenagers to vandalism and in adults to problems with self-destructive behavior. This is the opposite of the celebration of sacred time, for it looks to the material world to provide a spiritual comfort that the world is incapable of giving. To know true leisure, Pieper writes, is to possess "the power to overstep the boundaries of the workaday world and reach out to superhuman, life-giving existential forces which refresh and renew us before we turn back to our daily work."[15]

The medieval European world was filled with a dizzying array of such feast days. Each season was marked with days and even weeks of festivity when, in spite of their harsh living conditions, people were able to sing, feast, dance, and simply enjoy life. When the Puritans came, they purged the calendar of most of the old Catholic feasts and muted the others. In Puritan New England, even Christmas was barely acknowledged if it did not fall on Sunday. The mostly middle-class Puritans instituted regular six-day workweeks with no odd feast days and fostered a mentality that saw time as a strictly meted out commodity instead of a fluid and irregularly paced process punctuated by manifold opportunities to celebrate the sheer fact and glory of existence. Replacing red-letter days with "black-letter days," the Puritan influence, in the form of the Protestant work ethic, did much to douse the festal flame in our culture.[16] As we grew ever more secular, even such Sabbatarian rites as the Puritans left us eroded into mere diversions, Sunday excursions to theme parks or seaside resorts, pleasant enough activities but lacking the religious texture of full festal celebration. Between the Utilitarians, the Stalinists, and the Puritans, not to mention the workaholics who get promoted to management positions in corporations, it is no wonder many of us have no sense of celebration left at all.

And so, in the end, perhaps that is why we have managed to forget what true leisure was like. Like much else in our culture, leisure has lost its soul. When we get out of the habit of celebrating life itself, we can also lose heart. Our Sabbath celebrations are meant to encourage us. The word encourage, related to the French *coeur*, literally means "to put heart into."

Without the kind of regular encouragement that festal days can give us, the heart can go out of our lives; we become literally dis-couraged. We become cyborgs, automatons, extensions of our pagers, fax machines, and telephones. Our work is deprived of a larger context. When our lives and identities seem bound only by our vocations, we begin, as Albert Camus noted, to feel like Sisyphus, pushing our rock uphill from day to day, only to see it roll down again. (Though as Camus also noted, Sisyphus, as he walked down his hill in hell to begin his task again, was happy in his leisure time.) "If real leisure is deprived of the support of genuine feast days and holy-days, work itself becomes inhuman."[17]

So, the celebration of a ritual, which is another way of saying the experience of sacred time, is the celebration of all of life, the quotidian ways we earn our daily bread and also all those other elements of existence that extend beyond the mere struggle to survive. In the end, entering sacred time through prayer, meditation, ritual or festival is a way of saying yes to all life. *"To celebrate a festival means: to live out, for some special occasion and in an uncommon manner, the universal assent to the world as a whole."*[18] The gift of the ritual is the ability to leave it feeling that life as it is is "just so." Ideally, this is not just an affirmation of the comfortable status quo but of the suffering and shortcomings of life as well. The well-performed celebration leaves us saying, "Yes, life is worth living in spite of all the suffering connected with it." There is so much we can say no to in this life—the war, violence, crime, and greed of humanity, the apparently random cruelty of the natural world—and a cheap and easy cynicism about all this is a hallmark of our age; but those who experience the delights of the Sabbath will be able to say yes in spite of all, and to affirm the value and worth of living, even if they have had to fast and save in order to stage the festival itself.

The affirmation of life is possible because, in the ritual festive moment, we touch an eternity that knows no privation. Time, in its aspect as Chronos the devourer, disappears, and in its place we experience time as the prolific life giver that makes all possible and promises a continuance beyond this world of diminishing time. As Pieper puts it, in celebrating sacred time, "The constant attrition of our portion of vital substance is suspended for a moment by that 'resting Now' in which the reality of Eternity is revealed."[19] By exiting profane time and entering the liminal realm of sacred time, we shift our mental focus from the hurried world of our everyday lives and enter another rhythm, larger than that of our individual lives or even our society. By ritual gesture, costume, chant, dance, we mark the festal time by celebrating the fullness of being, its plenitude, not its scarcity. This is a world in which we are participants, but we are not its originators. As Pieper writes, "while man can make the celebration, he cannot make what is to be celebrated, cannot make the festive occasion and the cause for celebrating. The happiness of being created, the existential goodness of things, the participation in the life of God, the overcoming of death—all these occasions of the great festivals are gifts."[20]

This is a far cry from the time famine experienced by most people today. As Joost Merloo eloquently summed up, "Speed became the great killer of the technological age; the haste to nowhere is our escape from ourselves. Yet, the man who learns to meditate knows that he cannot waste time."[21] The value of ritual, well celebrated, is that in entering sacred time we see beneath the world of fleeting time another world of timelessness, a world that does not cease to exist when the celebration is over. Like an underground stream, sacred time is always present, even if hidden, always ready to be tapped into to quench the thirst of the time-weary traveler. Sacred time understood in this sense is potentially capable of sustaining perpetual festival, a life of unending celebration. Periodic festivals, weekly Sabbaths, yearly rites, holy days, and periods of meditation, prayer, or contemplation allow us to use our binocular vision to achieve a depth of insight into the nature of the life we are living. We may perhaps need only a bit of this sacred time to sustain us and allow us to always and everywhere say yes to life: a Sabbath day once a week, a half hour daily on a meditation mat, a yearly festival day, or a monthlong Ramadan. Just as we don't need to eat constantly in order to be nourished by our few daily meals, so too perhaps we don't need to be in perpetual meditation or ritual to benefit from the Sabbath experience. But we must have something, and in our culture, too often, we have nothing. So how can we live our way back into a Sabbath in the midst of a determinedly secular culture?

CHAPTER 7

Finding Sacred Time

AS PART OF MY RESEARCH for this book-length essay on time, I decided to take seriously, for one whole year, the biblical injunction to keep the Sabbath holy. I wanted to see what would happen if I devoted a portion of each week to finding sacred time, and this seemed like the most ready-to-hand way. But what form should my Sabbath keeping take?

Like most people today, I had allowed my Sabbath keeping to decline. Sunday morning ritual's had become a matter of pancakes, newspapers, an extra cup of coffee, and perhaps church if the spirit moved us. The afternoons often got cluttered with activities and the household chores that had piled up during the week. I usually tried to relax on Sundays, but, being a teacher, I always felt the pressure of Monday morning, so I often found myself prepping for class or reading student papers on Sunday evenings.

I was raised in a very religious family and had even spent two years studying for the Roman Catholic priesthood when I was of college age. My early life had been filled with the high ritual of the pre–Vatican II church, and a snatch of Latin or a whiff of incense can still carry me back to that ambience. As I remembered Sundays from my youth, I recalled the hurry to get to Mass, which was in many ways the high point of the week. The seasons of the liturgical year gave a rhythm to our family life as much as the seasons of the calendar year. I remembered Sunday mornings as times when we touched the *magnum mysterium*. The whole panoply of vestments, music, candles, and prayer colored my imagination, and Sundays became more vivid times thanks to them. There were certain pieces of music, like the *Cantate Dominum* or the *Victime paschale laudes* of Easter, that were taken out and put away from year to year like fine family heirlooms. These things had resonated deeply in me despite, or perhaps because of, the fact that they were in a language I didn't understand. Sunday afternoons back then were generally spent with the extended family. There were always dinners with relatives or family gatherings in parks with pickup ball games, and Sundays were always dominated by a general sense of what my Bavarian forebears would have called *Gemütlichkeit*, a cozy, close, relaxed atmosphere and general good feeling about life.

Somewhere along the way, that had changed, or I had changed, or both. Part of it, of course, had to do with changes in the Catholic Church's liturgy, changes of which I was particularly aware because I was a musician and had helped introduce the new liturgy back in the 1960s. Mystery was gone, community was in. Another part had to do with changes in myself and my situation. I had moved away from my extended family and had slipped away from Catholic practice. For a long period I had found more sense and meaning in Zen Buddhism; I had regularly practiced zazen and had attended Zen retreats. My contact with Catholicism was rather desultory, and yet, perhaps because I taught at a Catholic college, it had also become something I took for granted, as unnoticed as the fit of an old pair of shoes.

In addition to all the personal things that had eroded my Sabbath practice, changes had taken place in society as well over the past twenty or thirty years. With rare exceptions, people in my circle were not religious. If anything, religion was something of an embarrassment, something modern thinking people just didn't "do." To a large extent this uneasiness over religion may have come from the fact that religious rhetoric in the United States since about 1980 has been dominated by the religious right, and being "religious" became identified with a brand of conservative, almost backward and repressive social thinking. Combine that with the Middle Eastern religious zealotry that has led to so much terror in the world, and to call oneself religious was like being a flat-earther or member of the Michigan Militia.

And yet, a sort of hunger remained for something, even if I couldn't assign a name to it, so as I thought about how we have lost sacred time in the contemporary world, I decided to experiment with living my way back into a Sabbath practice that had ceased to mean much to me, just to see what changes would occur in me. I had learned much about the idea of Sabbath from my reading. My idea of what it should be was shaped by Hebrew tradition via my childhood upbringing in Catholicism.

In the beginning, Genesis tells us, the earth was a wasteland, a void over which the breath of God hovered. Then, through six days of work, God called forth the world and all that is in it. On the seventh day, however, he rested, and thus, Scripture says, he instituted the Sabbath. The Hebrew word *shabbath* literally means "rest." This day of repose was given by God as a sign of his covenant with the Jews, and it assumed tremendous importance for the chosen people. The rest that it demanded was absolute.

In Exodus 31:13–17, God tells Moses that this day is to be scrupulously work-free, so much so that anyone who profanes the holy day through work may be exiled or even put to death. The Hebrew Scriptures contain Sabbath-day prohibitions against travel, business, and even such apparently necessary labor as lighting cooking fires and candles. And yet, in spite of such restrictions, Isaiah 58:13 uses the Hebrew word *oneg*, delightful, to describe the day. Why? Rabbi Abraham Heschel, in his masterful meditation on the Sabbath, says the "rest" of the Sabbath means much more than simply not working. More positively, the Hebrew word *menuha* denotes a time of peacefulness, stillness, harmony, and repose.[1]

To celebrate the Sabbath fully, then, I would have to begin by resting completely from my labors. Only then could I experience the shift in attitude that would allow me to fully appreciate the sacredness of the day. The Scriptures make it clear that on this one day we are to set aside all the duties of the other six days of the week and take active delight in our own lives and in all of creation. Whereas during the rest of the week we struggle with the earth to make a living, on this one day we must simply stop and enjoy.

This is hard to do. The world Adam and Eve entered after the Fall, our world, is a realm of work and time. We must earn our bread by the sweat of our brow. We bring forth our children in labor. And in the end we are to die. Our world is clearly not the timeless pleasure garden of Eden. And yet, Scriptures tell us, by taking one day a week to celebrate life, we can learn that even this postlapsarian world of work and time is filled with divine presence and abundance. Stopping work one day a week makes us pay attention. At least one time a week we are reminded that the world we live in, as full of suffering as it can be, is also a world of joy and abundance. Rabbi Heschel said that Sabbath gives the Jews a foretaste of the world to come. The sweetness of the day of rest is supposed to teach us the taste of eternal life here and now. If we do not learn that lesson now, he writes, we will be unable to enjoy eternity later.

Not working, however, was only a beginning. Sabbath for the ancient and modern Jews was and is a day of active festivity rather than simple passivity. Far from being simply a time to recover from the hard labors of the week so one can go back to work refreshed, the Sabbath celebration is to be the highlight of the week. "For this reason, good food, drink, clothing, music, and aesthetics in general were all stressed for elevating the atmosphere and the human spirit on the Sabbath." Some rabbis even "regarded it as proper . . . to fast a goodly part of the week in order to conserve available funds for the family Sabbath dinner."[2]

In Scripture, there is a special Hebrew adjective for the Sabbath. *Qadosh*, translated as "holy," appears in the Decalogue only with regard to the Sabbath. "Remember the Sabbath day and keep it holy." All other days are referred to as *yom hol*, profane days.[3] In Jewish folk belief, according to Heschel, God gave human beings an additional soul (*neshamah yeterah*) at the beginning of the Sabbath. It is this expansion of the soul that makes the face shine in a special way on the sacred day. But more than that, Jews believe that on Sabbath not just the individual but the entire world receives an expanded soul. Sometimes Sabbath was envisioned as a personified guest who "comes periodically to 'visit' the profane world, as if to sanctify it by its sheer presence."[4] At other times, it was considered a bride. On that day, Heschel writes, observant human beings create a "palace in time," and though they are not in Paradise, Paradise is in them.

Building a palace in time requires a lot of work. The ancient Jews used specific rituals to carve out the sacred time.

Following Jewish tradition, Sabbath began at twilight, at the moment when three stars could be discerned in the sky. In ancient Judea the beginning of Sabbath was marked by the blowing of a ram's horn from the top of a village building six times. The first call stopped work in the fields. The second closed the shops in town. The third told people to remove food from ovens and to cease other preparatory activities, and the fourth through sixth blasts, blown in rapid succession, marked the actual entrance into the holy time.[5] The sacred time of celebration and delight ended twenty-four hours later with the *habladah*. With that ritual the celebrants recrossed the threshold back into the profane world of work and ordinary life, refreshed, renewed, and confident that beneath the workaday world of time there subsisted eternity.

By this time, I realized that the Sabbath must be lived, not merely studied, but how would I begin? This complex business of entering and leaving the sacred day is a tall order for a modern person. In the world I live in, no ram's horns are blown at sunset, and the momentum of the workweek scarcely ceases on any day, not even Saturday or Sunday. Still, I had hope. I decided to begin as Scripture suggested and convinced myself to stop working one day a week. I remembered the words of Rabbi Heschel: "Even when the soul is seared, even when no prayer can come out of our frightened throats, the clean silent rest of the Sabbath leads to a realm of endless peace, or to the beginning of an awareness of what eternity means."[6]

Quitting work one day a week was not as easy as I had hoped, however. Like most working people today, I felt "behind" most of the time. It was a foregone conclusion that much of Saturday would be spent working. Sunday, therefore, had become my catch-up day, when I could tie up all the loose ends of the week before. I had even been known to sneak into the office for an hour or two on Sunday afternoons just to get my notes together for Monday. When the idea first occurred to me to try to go for a whole year without working on Sundays, I had moments of panic. A voice inside my head said, "You'll fall further behind. Don't do it. You can't afford to." Most professionals will recognize this voice. Because there is no end to the work, we feel that the working must never end, too.

Thus, the first thing I came to understand about finding sacred or "Sabbath" time was that it called for extreme discipline. I began to comprehend the psychological necessity of the injunctions in Exodus and elsewhere in Scripture against performing even the most menial chores on the Sabbath and why in ancient times infractions were even punishable by death. The discipline required for Sabbath keeping is different from the discipline required during the week because it is, first of all, the hard discipline of doing nothing. This would not be so difficult if there were nothing to do, but in this world there is always something out there that needs attention. Nature abhors a vacuum, and a hole in one's schedule, especially if it is a day long, acts like a low-pressure area into which activities will leak if they sense the slightest opening. Because we live in a 24/7 culture, the Sabbath is no longer a reason for the world not to ask you to work. In fact, the requests sometimes come from surprising quarters. The faculty at my Catholic college were up in arms a few years ago when an upper-level administrator suggested holding classes on Sundays. His rationale was that rooms were not being used on Sunday afternoons and we could generate additional income if we held classes when both faculty and potential students had nothing to do.

I realized that the first discipline of Sabbath is learning to say no to the world of work. You must say no even to worthwhile projects needing your attention, even to things you or others may think are vital to your job, your profession, your life. As Josef Pieper explained, keeping the Sabbath needs, first of all, true leisure, and if leisure cannot be easily gotten because of the nature of your world, then you have to wrestle it from the grip of everyday life, even if this involves financial or personal risk.

At first, this was the most difficult part of keeping the Sabbath for me. Not only do I love my work, but I think it is work worth doing. My work involves talking and writing about literature, beauty, art, meaning. It is not as physically taxing as plowing fields or shoveling dung all week. Still, I had to learn to stop. When I forced myself not to work one day a week, I discovered that my world did not blow apart. In fact I had plenty of time to do what really needed doing, and eventually I realized I was coming to work on Monday mornings with more energy than I had brought with me for years. The first blessing of the Sabbath is recreation, in the sense of re-creation.

After I had succeeded in learning how not to work on Sundays, I decided to try a return to regular church going as a way of finding sacred time. I started my practice on the first Sunday of Advent, the beginning of the Catholic Church's liturgical year. This time of preparation coincides with the dwindling hours of daylight and leads to the winter solstice and Christmas.

My first reaction to attending Mass at my local Catholic parish was shock. After some years of private Zen-style practice, I had forgotten the hurly-burly of the typical Catholic parish's Sunday Mass, the barely organized chaos of squawling babies, visiting friends, chatty neighbors, strumming guitars, and rattling tamborines. People were dressed in "casual Friday" attire, some chewing gum, and they generally carried on as though they were at the local steakhouse and not the house of God. I did not know if I could stay the course for a whole year. It was only the first week of Advent, and I already felt I was in the wrong place.

And then the Mass began, and in the midst of the general roar, to my surprise, I was able to hear echoes of another time. The ancient Scripture and vestments, the promise of a better time, the sense of waiting that Advent implies: all that began to emerge from the noisy field, and though I did not feel altogether delivered from profane time (the reminders of the pancake supper, the Boy Scout meeting, and the school's fund-raiser kept distracting me), I nonetheless left Mass that day feeling that I had somehow begun a journey, however shakily, toward a new understanding of sacred time.

At the very least, I had begun paying attention once again to the movement of my religious tradition's liturgical year, and that forced me to pay more attention to the passing of the calendar year. Noticing the shortening hours of daylight in turn led me to contemplate more carefully the intricate connection between the liturgical calendar and the change of seasons.

I found myself paying more attention to the daily movement of the sun across the sky, to the monthly cycle of the moon, to the nightly procession of the constellations through the sky. Christianity is not the only tradition that expresses the idea of the sacredness of the seasonal cycle, of course. We human beings seem to take delight in contemplating the complexity of the universe around us and aligning our lives with its movement, but in our hurry we can forget to pay attention to the larger movements of the world we live in. After that first Advent Mass, I felt myself beginning to respond to the changing year in a new, or perhaps an ancient, way. If one of the sources of religion is a sense of awe in the face of the universe, then perhaps I was beginning to feel that awe again. Perhaps the sacred calendars of the world's religious traditions are simply ways to organize that awe, to call attention to different parts of it, and to arrange it through the year so it can be experienced in all its complexity.

At home, we lit the first candle of the Advent wreath on that same Sunday. This old Catholic tradition involves four candles arranged in a circle amid evergreen boughs. Each week until Christmas, with prayers, another candle is lit. I don't know how my son and wife felt about this ritual. We have other family rituals—meals, games, gatherings with friends—but none quite like this, where we opened the Bible to certain passages of the ancient Scriptures and read the prophecies of the coming Messiah. It was hard for me to do it without a sense of irony. Ours is the age of irony, when no one takes anything seriously, yet here we were lighting a purple candle in an Advent wreath.

The symbolism of light and flame is very powerful, and that alone seemed to mute the irony as the weeks of Advent went on. Darkness and light, fire and flame, what could be more archetypal? The liturgical year begins in darkness and moves toward the light. There is something hopeful in this idea. The Jewish Sabbath and the Celtic year also begin with the coming on of night. For the Jews, the new year begins with the autumn celebration of Rosh Hashanah; for the Celts with Samhain.[7] The increasing darkness of the season held the promise of light.

As the next three weeks unfolded, we lit more candles. In church, the large Advent wreath in the front was lit with great ceremony, usually by a parish family, and at home we continued weekly Bible readings. The first candle grew shorter, the others soon followed it. On the third Sunday of Advent, Gaudete Sunday, the candle was pink. On the fourth, we knew that in one week it would be Christmas. The days outside were growing darker and colder. Snow flew. We could hear the sounds of cars sliding through the icy streets. In Michigan, it is possible at this time of year to think that the world is entering a new Ice Age, that we will continue to spiral down into never-ending darkness. Yet we had those candles, weekly reminders that light would return.

As the four weeks of Advent passed, my experience of the liturgical year deepened. I still felt that much of the music at the church was insipid, that the sermons were a little too folksy, and yet I also kept finding nuggets of wisdom here and there that I could take with me into the week. "The people who lived in darkness have seen a great light" was a repeated refrain, and as I ruminated on the fact that the Christian year has a solar orientation, Christianity seemed more universal to me, more like one of the family of world religions than it usually does. One of the things that had always bothered me about Christianity was its insistence on its specialness, on its difference from other world traditions, but the universality of the solstice rites reminded me that even Christianity is but an expression of deeper, more universal truths. Perhaps the fundamental truth has to do with light overcoming darkness, in other words, with hope. I knew about some of the ways that sacred traditions around the world have celebrated the solstices and equinoxes. The Roman Saturnalia was a seven-day solstice festival that celebrated the victory of sunlight over the death of winter.[8] The Hopi year is also divided in two by the solstices, and in the Hindu epic *Ramayana*, the solar deity Rama defeats the earth-devourer Ravana at the exact moment of winter solstice. Worldwide, we seem to believe that light will triumph. Nature shows us the way.

By taking time to celebrate celestial events within a sacred calendar, we experience how our lives are connected to other lives and to the life of the universe itself. The modern mind tends to see the world as separated and fragmented, to see each individual's life as separate from all other lives. Celebrating sacred time, however, takes us into a world of connection and meaning. Thus we learn that the universe we experience is not neutral and it is not formless or even directionless. It has an order and a meaning. Participating in sacred time, even in a limited way, calls attention to that order, celebrates it, and puts our lives in line with it.

As Christmas approached, I decided to experiment with other solstice rituals. Having once done some research on Thomas Hardy's use of old British customs in his novels, I was able to dig up some material on mummers' plays and pulled together a script. On solstice night, we invited a few friends for a winter party, and in our living room, with quickly scraped-together props, we played out the drama of how Saint George, representing the sun, defeats the Turkish knight who represents the winter. My son, playing George, was more than happy to run me through with a wooden sword and stand in triumph on my Turkish corpse, until, with the rest of the cast, we stood up and sang carols, holding hands in front of the fire.

As I reflected on the experience later, I realized that recognizing the many connections between liturgies, folk ceremonies, and seasonal cycles must have been easier in an agricultural society. Mummers cannot go door to door in the suburbs, and in a world of electric light the solstice does not mean what it used to. And Advent, a time of waiting, seemed rather pointless in a society based on the immediate gratification of every impulse. Nonetheless, I was beginning to discover that keeping the Sabbath, even in the limited way I was trying to, could make me more conscious of a world of sacred time that formed a substrate to the time-bound and mundane world of my daily life. I felt I was tracing a path back to a way of being I had lost in recent years. Like everyone else, I had been going hell-bent into an open-ended future without much sense of where I was going or why. Now I was finding in the liturgical and seasonal cycle another idea of time and how it operates. I was coming to the realization that "progress," which so dominates our lives today, is not the only way of experiencing the passage of time. Living always in the future, we continually separate ourselves from the past, casting off the old, moving on. In observing sacred time, however, I was entering the past, building bridges to it, creating continuity, seeing connections among things rather than separations. I felt myself, however gingerly, stepping off the quickly moving conveyor belt of time and beginning to pause in the simple, timeless being that, having been, will always be.

The idea seemed oriental. In Hinduism, the world of clock time is regarded as an illusion. Everything, at every moment, is suffused with the fullness of being, Brahman. Therefore, even when outward forms change, nothing changes really. And therefore we can celebrate pure being. We may luxuriate in sacred time.

In Buddhism, this notion is found in the Zen attitude of focusing one's attention on the eternal now, living in the present, understanding that in being fully present, one is somehow outside of time even while participating in its ongoing flow, just as Chinese Taoist philosophy sees the eternal principles yin and yang operating in the vicissitudes of daily life.

Participating in the rituals of the Catholic Church, I realized, could give me access to that same sense. In the secular world, Sundays during Advent were the days when I would go the mall with the rest of the mob and fight over the latest toy. This year, however, I felt less frantic as Christmas approached. Newspapers and the evening TV news were filled with images of Christmas shoppers elbowing each other out of the way to get the latest toys, but I felt removed from that aspect of the season. As I watched the shopping melee unfold, I saw in it little of the sense of true celebration as Pieper defined it. However, I was finding contentment and joy in simple acts: lighting a candle, saying a prayer, or watching the sun come up, pale and white over the horizon, a little later each day.

I also found that it is extremely difficult to simply enjoy the season this way. The momentum of the culture tends the opposite way. Some years ago, friends of mine tried to counter the materialism of "the giving season" by declaring a gift-free Christmas. Instead of buying one another presents, the parents and children donated their money to worthwhile causes. On Christmas Day, they served dinner at a local soup kitchen. It seemed like a wonderful idea, and if it had been a made-for-TV movie it would have ended with everyone discovering the true meaning of Christmas, but the power of American culture is such that today, fifteen years later, the children still call it "the stupid Christmas" when they didn't get any gifts.

So, as Christmas approached, I discovered that this holiday, like every Sabbath, required discipline to keep me from losing focus on the meaning of the day. The discipline of the previous Advent Sabbaths I had kept made it easier to keep the real spirit of Christmas. It had a cumulative effect, as it were. For some years, I had been a Christmas and Easter

Christian, someone who popped into church on those two days because of a vague urge to connect with something I once knew. Now I was beginning to understand that dipping in and out of the liturgical year that way was sort of like listening to a "Fifty Great Moments in Music" recording. We can listen to only the highlights, but often the greatness of the musical moment depends on what comes before and after. Handel's Hallelujah Chorus or the initial four notes of Beethoven's Fifth are great, but disconnected from their context we may be left wondering what all the fuss is about. So, too, I was rediscovering, with the liturgical year. A temporal rhythm is set up when we keep the Sabbath regularly. The weekly celebrations build up to special days like Christmas that serve as emotional high points the way that unresolved chords or motifs in music achieve emotional intensity the moment they are resolved and we understand, with a sort of "aha," what all the development has been leading up to.

Christmas this year came and went with special meaning. Outwardly, we did most of the same things we do every year—went to Mass on Christmas Eve, got up early, opened presents, drove off to see family and friends—but inwardly I felt a different resonance. The gestalt was shifting.

New Year's came and we turned over the calendar. Time was passing. Five days after New Year's Day came Epiphany, January 6, the date Western Christians celebrate the visit of the Three Kings to Bethlehem to see the infant Jesus. Traditionally the feast has been important because it commemorates the introduction of Christianity to the Gentiles. This year, however, I found it significant because of the name itself. The word epiphany comes from the Greek *epi* + *phanein*, to show, manifest, reveal. It is used to mean a moment when some inner reality shines forth, in this case, the divinity of

Jesus shining through his earthly form. As I reflected on this feast, I could not help associating this with the Hindu idea of Brahman, the great source of Being from which all things come and the energy that flows through all beings, including humans. The epiphany of Jesus, I thought, is the epiphany of us all, for divinity is within us all. The Hindus say *tat tvam asi*, thou art that, by which they mean all of us have that spark of divinity within us waiting to shine forth. It will manifest itself to those who can see. I also reflected that the Christian Epiphany is celebrated as the hours of daylight increase, thus its "shining forth" continues the seasonal cycle as the celebration of the birth of Jesus had only two weeks before. These liturgical mileposts had the odd effect of making me more aware, from day to day, that the sun was coming up earlier. As I walked the mile to work each day, I noticed that the sun was moving, slowly but surely, higher in the sky, light triumphing over the darkness of a Michigan winter.

The next high holy season was Lent. It began with Mardi Gras, also known as Shrove Tuesday. The two names underscore the paradoxical nature of the day. As Mardi Gras, or fat Tuesday, it is a carnival, a farewell to meat (from the Latin *carne*, flesh or meat, and *levare*, to remove). In the Middle Ages, Christians were forbidden to eat meat on Ash Wednesday and Fridays during the forty days of Lent. The Catholic Church still follows these old rules, and, as part of my liturgical year, I intended to as well.

Mardi Gras harks back to the Roman Feast of Fools, a day when normal social conventions were set on their ears. On this day, servants became masters, prisoners were released, and a general sense of misrule prevailed. The Feast of Fools continued into the Middle Ages, sometimes celebrated with the appointment of a Pope of Fools or a Lord of Misrule and often including a *Missa Asinorum*, an "Ass's Mass," which featured leading a donkey into church and then a bawdy parody of the ritual of the Mass. The day's original function was as a social safety valve. In a rigidly hierarchical society like ancient Rome or medieval Europe, these periodic festival days could release social tensions that might otherwise explode in revolutions.

Today, this topsy-turvy day has become a day of mere excess in many places, most famously in New Orleans. It is often merely an excuse for drunkenness and brawls rather than true celebration and revelry. In a society like ours, which seems rather slack and open, I wondered, what function does Mardi Gras serve? In an era of twenty-four-hour-a-day, seven-day-a-week entertainment options, is a Mardi Gras even necessary? In a sense, in our commercial culture, every day is Mardi Gras, a day for turning over structures and elevating fools to high office. Not only that, it occurred to me that an upside-down day of carnival makes sense only if it is followed by a period of austerity, and with our Mardi Gras, the only austerity we may practice afterward is a morning of hangover remedies. After that, life returns to its normal indulgence. I skipped New Orleans this year.

Instead, I focused on the other name for the day, Shrove Tuesday, the day when medieval Christians would go to have their sins forgiven through the sacrament of penance. We have little sense today of the need to be shriven from our sins. Not only has the sense of sin been done away with, but it often seems that we have tossed out the idea of taking personal responsibility for our actions at all. Shrove Tuesday, a day of confession and admission of guilt, seemed to me wildly anachronistic in an age when even national leaders caught red-handed seem to manage no more of a *mea culpa* than a weak "mistakes were made," as if no one in particular really made them. In an age when culpability seems to have devolved into legal technicality, I wondered, what meaning can Shrove Tuesday have?

Nonetheless, I set aside the day to contemplate my sins. I spent some time examining my conscience, trying to assess just what responsibility I may have had over the past year for adding to the world's store of pain and suffering. I sat down and thought about conscience, guilt, responsibility, the way I was living my life. Do I really follow through on the values I profess? Do my actions match my words? Do I live what I teach others? Can I look myself in the face in the mirror and say, yes, I have managed to reach midlife without violating the principles I believed in when I was younger? To set aside a day for this can be a withering and humbling experience. Socrates said it best: the unexamined life is not worth living. And yet who normally has time? We are too busy thinking about the future to worry about the past. At most, we might examine the past to avoid making future mistakes, but mostly we feel that what's done is done. Yet I discovered that the examination of conscience, a practice we used to do regularly back in grade school, serves a vital function. It is good to sit down and ask yourself the hard questions. The Jews do it each year with the Day of Atonement, asking forgiveness of those they have wronged.

Even though I did not get formally shriven on Shrove Tuesday, I discovered that examining one's conscience is also examining one's consciousness. As late as the 1600s these two etymologically related words were practically synonymous. Once, to have a conscience was to be conscious of one's life, one's world, one's proper role in society and how to comport oneself toward other people. The sting of conscience, the bite of remorse, prodded you to a higher level of consciousness of the ethical nature of the life you were living. By doing away with conscience, by calling it an antiquated concept—by, in effect, saying that people are shaped only by their environments and social conditions and have no responsibility for their personal actions, not even for murders they commit— we modern people have done away with one of the greatest prods we have toward personal growth. Shrove Tuesday has no place in an "I'm OK, you're OK" world. A "call to conscience" can even be seen as somewhat regressive, old-fashioned, and unenlightened. But the alternative is to live without reflecting on the moral and ethical relations we have with others, without considering our place in the web of ethics or moral values. Though I wore no sackcloth or ashes, I ended Shrove Tuesday humbled at my shortcomings.

On Ash Wednesday, I readied myself for Lent. In my youth, Ash Wednesday was a somber day, marked with black vestments, dark funereal candles, and, of course, the dispensing of ashes. I remembered the gritty crush of ash as the priest's thumb smeared a black cross on my forehead with the grim admonition, "Remember, man, that thou art dust and unto dust you shall return." It was a chilling reminder of death as the church entered the season of Lent.

For many years, I had not participated in Ash Wednesday services, nor did I keep Lent, but as part of my liturgical year I decided to go back to it. I attended the Ash Wednesday Mass at my college. More people than I had expected were at the service, colleagues and students, Catholics and non-Catholics. I was reminded in an odd way of the scene in Nathaniel Hawthorne's "Young Goodman Brown" where Brown shows up at the witches' Sabbath to see his friends and neighbors gathered to celebrate their secret lives, only my experience was the opposite of Brown's. These people, whom I knew only in a professional capacity, also had a secret life of the spirit about which we rarely spoke, a life of deep religious belief. It was moving to see these people gathered together to receive the mark of ash on their foreheads. Most surprising of all, perhaps, was to see a local Protestant minister there. A friend of mine and an associate pastor at a liberal church, he had become intrigued with the idea of Ash Wednesday's dramatic gesture of humility and repentance and had come to join the service at the invitation of a Catholic friend.

Somewhat to my dismay, I discovered that in the church, as in the rest of society, death has become something of a taboo subject, a downer. The ashes were still there, of course, but instead of the stern yet powerful reminder of mortality in the spoken formula, there was now a bland admonition to "Go forth and keep the teachings of the gospel." One still came out with a spot on the forehead, but some of the punch was lost. The new Ash Wednesday liturgy seemed disconcertingly upbeat, as though the Lent of old had somehow become "Lent lite." Still, there was enough of the *memento mori* in it to make me reflect on the end of my life, and the priest's sermon reminded me that Lent required discipline and humility, and I resolved that I would be open to wherever the spirt led me through the next forty days.

I had decided to follow church practice and fast during Lent, starting on Ash Wednesday. I had not fasted in a long time, and as my stomach growled during the Mass, I remarked to myself how long it had been since I had known hunger. Of course I had been hungry before dinner, but I knew that my hunger could be easily satisfied at any time. This being the United States, one is never far from food. Restaurants, supermarkets, and convenience stores are open twenty-four hours a day to satisfy our appetites. What is the point of fasting in a land of constant feast?

The first thing I noticed as Lent began was that I began to think more about food than I usually did. In fact, the hungrier I got, the more I found myself thinking about the whole business of eating. Eating, I discovered, can reveal one of the great underlying mysteries of life itself: that life feeds on death. In order for me to live, something else, even if it is only a carrot, has to give its life for me. This, said Joseph Campbell, is one of the great wellsprings of world mythology, for it is nothing less than the realization of the interconnectedness of life and death.

I also became more aware of how we take food for granted in our culture. Years ago, an Italian nun was a student in one of my courses. She had spent some years working as a missionary in Africa. One day, during a discussion of American television, she became quite heated about something she had seen the night before. A story on the evening news about starvation in Africa had been placed back to back with a gourmet cat food commercial. The almost surreal juxtaposition of these two bits of video was, in her word, obscene. She was appalled at the inequity of a world where the cats of one country can be fed select bits of prime tuna while millions of people starve on other continents. Perhaps it took an outsider to point out to me what should have been obvious: we have grown so used to the abundance of food we enjoy in the United States that most of us can no longer conceive of real hunger. We have become an obese nation. We get our gratification through food ("You deserve a break today"), and many of us eat compulsively, even when we are not hungry. A quick glance at the magazine rack in the grocery store reveals that we are a nation obsessed with dieting and losing weight. But this is not the same thing as religious fasting.

Voluntary fasting exists in many traditions. The most well known is the monthlong fast of Ramadan, practiced by Muslims. Ramadan begins in the ninth month of the Islamic calendar when the first sliver of the new moon is seen in the sky. From dawn to sunset, believers are not to let any food pass their lips. Hinduism, too, has a fasting tradition. It is famous for its ascetics who deny themselves food and drink and otherwise chastise the body. The Buddha, on his course to enlightenment, is said to have fasted for seven years, and Jesus, before beginning his public ministry took himself to the desert to fast and pray for forty days. Somehow denying ourselves food for the body results in our getting food for the soul.

For my Lenten practice, I decided to skip lunches and also to abstain from meat on Fridays and to give the money I would have spent on those meals to international famine relief. It was a modest fast, but, even so, the pangs of physical hunger, incurred voluntarily, seemed to quicken my spiritual impulse. There are surely some physiological explanations for this. Perhaps in our ancestral environment where food was scarce, those survived best whose senses were acute enough to see and smell out food. The drive to satisfy hunger is a powerful one, and purposely denying oneself food makes the senses more keen, which in turn may feel like a higher level of awareness and consciousness.

As the days of Lent went on, my fasting led me to other thoughts. I was reminded how much we are driven by all our appetites. Because I had never experienced real hunger, I was not fully aware of how appetite-driven I was. Human beings have appetites for power, for wealth, for control, for earthly life itself. In Hinduism, there are three impediments to salvation, the three gunas. They are appetites for power, for laziness, and finally for being itself. The appetite for power, called *rajas*, is personified in the Hindu epic *Ramayana* as the demon Ravana who flies over the earth devouring people, animals, and whole kingdoms with his ten heads. He is an eating machine, and what he eats he controls. In the end, this appetite leads to his own destruction at the hands of Rama, one of the earthly incarnations of Vishnu the sustainer. Our hungers, if they are misplaced or if they are after the wrong things, destroy us in the end.

The hunger pangs I endured with ritual fasting reminded me that our appetites can be controlled. This is an important message in our society, which seems to run on the principle of instant gratification. We are encouraged to satisfy not just our appetites for food but our cravings for every other material pleasure as well, and the sooner the better. Hidden in all of these messages is a subtle but pervasive assumption that if we don't seize the day, the moment will pass and we will be deprived forever.

The lesson of Lent, therefore, is that when we learn to control our appetites, we can discover other dimensions of our being than the merely physical. To undertake the discipline of Lent is ultimately to discipline the self to keep all one's appetites in perspective. Conquering the appetite for food should lead us to contemplate how much we are driven by other cravings.

Like the other seasons of the liturgical year, Lent also seems to correspond well with the climatic season. We participate in the dearth of winter, even if we don't have to. But, as is true of the earth, last season's seeds lie dormant, awaiting the moment to spring to life.

That time comes, of course, during Holy Week, the climax

of the Christian liturgical year. In just three intense days, the heart of the Christian mystery is lived out through rituals that take believers back into the time of the death and resurrection of Jesus, and all of this takes place as the earth itself is showing signs of renewed life.

The Catholic Good Friday service still includes the veneration of the cross, a relic of the Middle Ages that the Puritans regarded as idolatrous and took great pains to stop in sixteenth-century England. In this ritual, known in ancient times as "creeping to the cross," the priest and people venerate the crucifix, often kneeling and kissing the feet of the Christ figure. In medieval times, believers crept forward barefoot and on their knees. After the veneration, Christ, in the form of the consecrated host, was processed through the church and symbolically "buried" in a special Easter sepulcher until Easter morning.[9] Through this theatrical and magical liturgy, people could participate dramatically in the events commemorated at that time in the liturgical year. At the very least, Good Friday services today include a reading of the gospel narrative of the Crucifixion and the singing of such funereal music as Mozart's *Requiem*.

I attended the Good Friday service at my local church. In a slow, somber procession, the members of the congregation went forward to venerate the cross, stooping to kiss the feet of the figure of Jesus. It was a humbling experience, for we are not used to bowing before anything anymore. But, I thought, perhaps this, the great mystery of suffering and death, is something worthy of adoration, or at least of awestruck humility. In our modern hubris we think we will one day overcome death through our medicine, but on Good Friday I found it oddly liberating to bow down before its inevitability and kiss its feet.

These *memento mori* rituals must strike many people today as "morbid." We have become unaccustomed to death. When it does enter our lives, it usually comes in a high-tech hospital where every heroic measure is taken to preserve life. Today death is often regarded more as a failure of technology and science than as the inevitable culmination of every human pilgrimage. Looked at the modern way, every death is failure rather than a fulfillment. Death, in a materialistic culture, is the worst evil, an absolute end because the death of the physical body is the absolute extinction of the self. Rather than face that, we try not to think about it. We have become a death-denying culture.

And yet, on Good Friday I realized that much can be gained by remembering our mortality. The ancient *memento mori* rituals, or the meditation on the seven last words of Christ, are sobering, but they bring into stark relief the life choices that lie before us.

I had not meditated on the cross for some time, so as part of my Good Friday observance I looked at some historic images of the Crucifixion. In paintings, we generally see Jesus hung on the cross, with the two thieves on either side of him. At the foot of the cross is often a skull and a few bones, a reminder that Golgotha, the hill on which Jesus was crucified, was also known as the place of the skull. In medieval legend, as told in the *Cursor Mundi* (c. 1300), the skull and bones at the foot of the cross were those of Adam himself, and the wood of the cross was hewn from a tree descended from the tree of life, seeds of which Adam's son Seth smuggled out of Paradise. Standing below the cross, in various postures of grief, are the mother of Jesus and John the beloved disciple, as well as other figures like soldiers and hangers-on.

At the center of it all stands the cross. In the early days of

Christianity, the cross was not emphasized as a symbol because the new religion was focused on the Resurrection, not the death of Jesus. Eventually, however, it became the central symbol of Christianity. The cross is extremely simple as a geometric figure, much simpler than, say, the black and white fish-shaped figures of the Tao. A horizontal line crosses a vertical line. I think the reason the symbol became so powerful is that we experience so much of life as dichotomy, and we continuously struggle with contradiction as part of our everyday lives. On either side of Jesus hangs a thief, one good, one bad. We, too, are daily "crucified" or suspended between good and evil. We are faced with difficult decisions, caught between optimism and despair over the human condition, between repentance and hardened cynicism. Like us, Jesus hangs and suffers between the earth and sky, between good and evil, between female and male (his mother and John), between life and death, between the sun and moon, light and dark. To be crucified between all these opposites is the condition of human life. Like Jesus, we often feel forsaken, abandoned by God.

In some depictions of the Crucifixion, the corpus is horribly realistic. In the old mission churches in the Spanish southwest of the United States, the tortured body of Jesus is shown without mercy, twisted and bloody, a terrifying depiction of the reality of human suffering and death.

And yet there is hope in all this. In many medieval paintings, a pelican nests atop the cross. In legend, the female pelican was believed to pierce her own breast to feed her young with her blood. Other medieval images show Jesus hanging from a tree that sprouts fresh green leaves and abundant fruit, to show that the tree of death is also the tree of life. The meditation on the cross on Good Friday shows us the inevitability of suffering. It shows us how we must die, but it also shows us how we must live, and ultimately it tells us that living well and dying well may be the same thing.

Holy Saturday brings a brief fallow time, a day of rest from the high drama of Good Friday, and a pause somewhat like a soft passage in a symphony before the finale, or like a time of germination, seed time, incubation, in which something will come to life in the Easter vigil, for me the highlight of the liturgical year.

The Catholic Easter vigil begins with the blessing of the fire. A new flame is kindled in the darkness, and from that flame the large paschal candle is lit. From that candle, a flame is passed to small candles held by the congregation until soon the nave of the church is shimmering in golden candlelight. The priest or cantor chants the beautiful *Exultet*, a recitation of the Creation story through the flood, and we are reminded how this candle, the work of the bees, brings light to the world. According to ancient ritual, the numbers of the year are carved into the candle's wax, and grains of incense are set in an inscribed cross to represent the wounds of Christ. Also inscribed on the cross are the ancient Greek letters alpha and omega, representing the beginning and the end of time. And so profane time and sacred time are fused together in one image, the ever-burning flame. After the long dearth and darkness of Lent, the church bursts back into light and music with the *Gloria in excelsis Deo*.

The ninth-century *Quem quaeritis trope*, a primitive enactment of the Easter gospel, seized on this moment, and from it eventually flowed the rest of European drama.

"Whom seek ye?" the angel asked the women at Jesus' tomb.

"Jesus of Nazareth," they replied.

"He is not here; he is risen from the dead."

After the dearth of winter, spring has come; out of death, there has come life.

After Easter, the liturgical year slows down. Ascension Thursday follows forty days after Easter Sunday, and Pentecost comes ten days after that. As I continued to follow the liturgical year, even these relatively minor days took on a new meaning for me. Both days suggested an end to time. Ascension Thursday, when Jesus left his followers with the promise to return again, and Pentecost, which filled them with the unpredictable energy and power of the Holy Spirit, both point toward an end of time, when history will be finished. Thinking about these days in that context gave me new perspective on the life and times I found myself living in, for, from the sacred perspective, time had a direction, goal, and purpose it otherwise lacked.

After this, the church year enters what is known as Ordinary Time.

During Ordinary Time, my search for sacred time moved away from the high drama of the church year and became more personal. All through this year, I had tried to combine my church going with a Zen practice I had always felt was perfectly compatible with my Catholicism. I was introduced to Zen-style meditation by a Jesuit priest who had studied in the Orient and who had incorporated zazen into his own spirituality. At the time, in the late 1960s, this was considered pretty avant-garde, and I found it intriguing enough that within a few years I adopted zazen as a method of calming and centering myself. That practice led me further into Buddhist readings, beginning with the works of D. T. Suzuki and Shunryu Suzuki and then into readings of the ancient writers, especially the works of Dogen, the twelfth-century founder of the Japanese Soto school of Zen. This in turn led me to attend Zen retreats at temples here in the United States and also in Japan. I had set aside a room in the house for practice.

In the past few years the demands of the outside world were so overwhelming that my zazen practice had become sporadic and scattered, and so I used this liturgical year to return to regular practice. Like many others, I found that the Zen approach to life provided a wonderful antidote to the frantic and fragmented modern world. The half hour or so I would spend on the *zabuton*, or cushion, several times a week became a sacred time for me, when I could touch, for a moment, a line between consciousness and unconsciousness and experience a sort of focused awareness of what was around me without any nagging sense that I should get up and do something. The Zen emphasis on living in the present allowed me to put aside, for a while, the weight of the future that constantly presses against us. It allowed me a respite from the pangs of time famine.

Gradually, as my practice continued and I was tossing around the ideas for this book, I think I began to understand more clearly what the ancient masters meant about not trying for anything in your zazen practice. Like everyone, I spent most of the week reaching after a future that wasn't there, living in advance of myself, planning, implementing plans, and then planning some more for events that became increasingly urgent as they came closer. When I first began zazen practice over twenty years ago, I think I was reaching after something, too, trying for "growth" in my spiritual life, thinking of enlightenment as something I needed more of, not being able to just sit because I thought there was supposed to be some point to the sitting.

Now, however, in the context of trying to experience the

sacredness of time, I understood better that just sitting is enough. I recalled that the first requirement of entering sacred time, whether you find it in a church, in a synagogue, or on a zabuton, is to accept the gift of existence. During this part of my year, I carved out a few days for myself and took a tent up into a wilderness area along the shore of Lake Michigan. There I stripped myself of as many accoutrements of what we usually call civilization as I could and spent three days wandering with compass and water jug in the sand dunes and forest. At sundown, I formed the sand atop an isolated dune into a makeshift pillow and simply sat facing west, accepting the tremendous gifts of the breeze over my face, the sand beneath my legs and bottom, the sound of waves breaking against the shore, and the cool heat of the orange sun as it descended before me. I sat that way until the western sky was dark and the first stars appeared above me. I felt, at that moment, that life itself was enough. There was nothing more to reach for.

So, the summer of my year's experiment passed, and in early September I noticed the subtle changes in the colors of the trees that signaled the beginning of autumn. By October, the air had acquired its autumnal snap, and the leaves made a riot of color. In October, we celebrated Halloween, the ancient Celtic feast of Samhain, when the gateway between this world and the next was believed to be briefly open. It was followed by All Saints' Day, November 1, and I recalled reading the ancient martyrologies when I was young and wondered who today would be willing to die for their beliefs. There was no end of action heroes, I reflected, in movies starring Sylvester Stallone and Arnold Schwarzenegger, but where were the heroes of conscience who had more than a hyperfetishized torso to recommend them? Where were the saints and holy fools who lived with one foot in the realm of sacred time?

Then came All Souls' Day, on November 2. On that day I called to mind all the dead from my life: my father, the older sister I had never known, friends who had died of accident and overdose, and the long procession of those who had gone before me into the dark land from which none has yet returned. Where exactly was this land? I don't think even many theologians still believe there is a literal place up in the sky called heaven. The ancient Irish believed the souls of the dead went west over the great sea, a belief that must have made my Irish ancestors' departure for the New World more poignant. Many Native Americans believed in a land of the dead that is remarkably like the one the living inhabit. And in African tribes, the dead form an integral part of the life of the village and are regularly included in feasts and rites. The ancient Romans believed that their children were reincarnations of ancestors who had waited in the Elysian Fields until a suitable body was ready. All Souls' Day reminded me that what lives on from generation to generation is not just the DNA that is replicated but something more. The dead billions who went before us, now nameless and forgotten, must be recalled from time to time, for without them we would not be here, and one day each of us will join that long procession.

Before these thoughts could weigh too heavily on me, the year came around again to Advent. As one liturgical year ended, the next began, forming a seamless cycle that has recurred as long as people have kept the Sabbath. I had discovered many things during my liturgical year. First of all, I realized that the liturgical year is not a simple circle. We do not simply repeat the same spiritual round every year. Rather, following the liturgical year through a lifetime is like walking a path that spirals up a mountain, and as we ascend we pass above the same landscape again and again, but always with a higher perspective, a view that sees farther and is more encompassing. This is the gift of keeping the Sabbath regularly; this is what we receive from the discipline of "doing nothing" on certain days.

I discovered that when we keep the Sabbath on a regular basis, we learn to live our lives with quite a different sense than if we treat every day the same. Sabbaths or holy days/holidays impart a different emotional feel than ordinary days. They mark epochs, years, turning points, and cycles and allow us to recognize and honor the various levels, depths, and colors of our lives. Sabbath keeping allows us to experience life as if it were a symphony with fast and slow movements. Through observance of holy days, the year attains a dramatic rhythm full of emotional intensity.

In our multicultural society, one of the problems we face is whose Sabbaths to celebrate, or to put it another way, whose religious traditions do we honor? In a mostly Christian society, we have privileged Christian holidays like Christmas by closing government offices and banks on those days, while we have ignored other traditions. No government office closes, for example, on Buddha's birthday, celebrated in Asia in May. Our decision, based on the principle of the separation of church and state, is to really celebrate no one's holy days. After my liturgical year, however, I would like to recommend that we celebrate them all, every tradition, make every day in school a feast of some kind. In December, celebrate Christmas, Hanukkah, and Kwanza. Honor Ramadan and solstices. The other alternative, to celebrate no one's holy days, is to risk losing the spirit of sacred time altogether, to risk forgetting how to celebrate life at all. If that happens, then we will be left only with the sort of pseudofestivity that surrounds purely secular occasions, events that are marked with some of the external signs of a Sabbath, like taking time off work, but lack the inner spirit of sacred time. In our society, we have replaced the real spirit of sacred time with mere sensationalism, entertainment, and spectacle that fail to get at the heart of existence itself. In a materialistic society, writes French philosopher Jean Guitton, we often try to compensate for our lack of inner spirit with material objects. This is the basis of all our advertising, which tries to sell us love, prestige, identity, even time, in the form of the next new and improved consumer product. For Guitton, this is the very definition of sin, trying to make the created stand for the creator. "In order to compensate for inner emptiness and to prevent what he loves from slipping away from him, he projects the sensory object into infinity, worships it, and thus his error becomes his god."[10]

Blessed with a standard of living unprecedented in history, with a plethora of material goods and a longer life span than previous generations, we should be in a state of constant celebration of life's abundance, and yet the true celebratory spirit, in Josef Pieper's sense, seems in short supply. Perhaps the spirit of the Sabbath needs to be reinvented or rediscovered by individuals and the culture at large. This may call for creativity and imagination so that new forms may come to be and old forms may be reinvigorated. Some will find the experience of sacred time in the old ways; others will invent new ones. What is called for in either case is an openness to the spirit of sacred time. If we can find that openness, then who knows what will come in moments of true inspiration? When the soul is quieted and open and receptive to the abundance of being, anything may happen.

Many believe there is only one way to celebrate the Sabbath, but in truth there are infinite ways, for the experience of sacred time is the experience of being itself and cannot be limited by historic forms. The spirit will manifest itself in manifold ways, and over time old traditions will be reshaped and new ones will come to be. The important thing is to stop, be receptive, and find the fine balance point between tradition and innovation. "What matters," wrote Pieper in *In Tune with the World*, "is not mere preservation and conservation of the old forms of Sabbath observance, but a constant succession of new, creative reshapings which give contemporaneity to the content of the festivals."[11] This is important to remember in a time when hidebound conservatives will tell us there is only one way, invariably theirs, to celebrate being. We must be faithful to the past, in our Sabbath observance, but as Jean Guitton remarks, "What beclouds the issue of tradition is our readiness to believe that faithfulness to the past consists in maintaining against all obstacles the forms, images and laws of a bygone period; actually, we should be concerned to rediscover the spirit of a past period and to create for it new molds and translations that are scaled to the present. When this is not done, the Church declines and the State is corrupted."[12]

In other words, sacred time must be honored, for in finding sacred time, we find ourselves.

The End of Time

THIS BOOK BEGAN WITH an examination of how we are caught up in the minutiae of modern daily life. It has explored how religious traditions, rituals, and spiritual practice can give us access to sacred time so that we may feel connected to a source of life greater than ourselves. But there is a danger, I think, that the search for sacred time can degenerate into mere "feel-goodism" in which our goal is simply to escape the real problems of the world in favor of being perpetually blissed out. If we are not careful, we may separate or compartmentalize sacred time and thus divide our Sabbath practice from our weekday lives, not feeling the relationship between the two. The search for sacred time takes place within the context of historical time, and somehow we must return to history.

The world's religious traditions show us that our single lives are not enough. We live in a social context and in a cosmic context. Without connection to a larger scheme of things, our daily lives become lonely, isolated, brief and tragic, ending with the finality of death. A major part of anyone's sense of sacred time in the modern world ought to be a firm belief that from day to day one's personal and individual life is part of the larger life of the world, that one is dancing in time with the universe, not just in ritual moments but in every action. This is a tall order. Most of us would be happy just to get a little more free time. Yet it is a fundamental and necessary part of a religious worldview to believe deep down in the core of our being that our lives have a point and purpose within a larger scheme of things.

When it comes to the ultimate end or purpose of time, however, modern science seems to offer us only a vision of a mechanism winding down or blowing up some billions of years hence. Cosmologists tell us that time began some 15 billion years ago with the big bang, and it will ultimately end in one of two ways. Either the impetus from the universe's initial explosion will continue moving matter (and thus time) outward forever, or someday the combined gravitational attraction of the stars and planets will equal and then exceed the force that moves the galaxies apart, and the universe will begin drawing itself back in again toward the center. Some theorists believe that time will then begin running literally backward.[1] Others believe that the experience of time will be roughly the same in the contracting universe as it is now. Still others honestly don't know what to think. Not that it will matter much to those of us here on earth. Scientists also predict that our sun will likely blow up in about 5 billion years, taking earth and most of the solar system with it. For us, time will have ended long before. Modern science's vision of time makes me think that Voltaire was correct. At the end of *Candide*, a character opines that human beings are like rats riding in the bilge of a great ship of whose direction and destination they are ignorant.

When we look to religion to supply a larger meaning to our lives, however, we run into other problems. Today the world is ripped apart by religious differences, not just in the tension between the Islamic world and the West but across the globe. Protestants face off against Catholics in Northern Ireland, Orthodox Christians against other Christians in the Balkans, while Hindus fight Muslims in India. The more fundamentalist and thoroughgoing a people's belief, it seems, the more likely it is that their sacred or religious view of history leads to strife. Those who profess to live in sacred time, who read Scripture, pray daily, and refer everything to their vision of eternity, can come to see themselves as divine agents acting for God in history. The more religious their worldview, it seems, the more likely they are to leave a trail of blood behind them.

So how do we negotiate this perilous passage? How can we grant the fundamentalist's major premise that modern secular materialist life has major shortcomings, that it tends to suffocate the life of the spirit, and yet avoid the fundamentalist's error that says that my God is the only God, my way is the only way? Throughout this book, I have taken the Middle Ages as a touchstone, using its monasticism and books of hours as examples of how people live in an age of faith. I have critiqued the rise of secularism, materialism, and modernism and have called for a return to a spiritual vision and way of life. Is it possible, however, to possess a sacred view of time and the world without crashing on the reef of fundamentalism? The Middle Ages, for all its faith, was also a time of tremendous ignorance and prejudice.

I believe it is not only possible to integrate faith and knowledge, but I believe that our age must be another of the world's great ages of faith. But the faith that is called for today is not the easy faith of jihad or crusade. The simple-minded or desperate can always be convinced to kill and die for their gods. This historical moment calls on us to discover a faith that is deeper and more difficult. Today, or very soon, we absolutely must learn to believe that the divinity of the entire universe reveals itself in all that is good in all of the world's religious traditions, in all that calls us to treat our fellow human beings and the universe itself with greater love and compassion and dignity. We must also believe, contrary to so much evidence in the world today, that the human race as a whole is moving toward greater understanding of itself and the universe it inhabits, and that perhaps the next phase of our history must be to reintegrate the spirit into our understanding of the physical universe.

Some 3,500 years ago, the great prophet Zarathustra proposed a grand vision of the purpose of time and history and the universe itself. The religion named after him, Zoroastrianism, was probably the world's first religion to have a systematized eschatology—that is, a vision of the end of time—that included the possibility of human beings' allying themselves with a principle of light or a principle of darkness, on the basis of which they would be judged for eternity. The whole universe, the Zoroastrians believed, was engaged in a massive struggle between the forces of dark and the forces of light, a struggle that, in the end, the light would win.[2]

This Zoroastrian view of time, to me, represents a massive leap of human consciousness. Prior to Zarathustra, the religion of Mesopotamia consisted of a fatalistic and apparently endless round of propitiating unpredictable gods and goddesses. Time went nowhere and life went only into a grim and shadowy underworld. Zarathustra was the first to offer a vision of a future significantly different from—and better than—the present. He was not alone. His vision is similar to the idea developing in Buddhism at roughly the same time that foresees a gradual progression of all sentient beings in the universe toward an age of full enlightenment at which time the Buddha Maitreya will return to lead the whole cosmos into nirvana. Zarathustra's eschatological view is also an obvious precursor of the messianic ideal in Judaism and of Christian eschatology.[3]

This vision of an end and purpose to time enables those who share it to think beyond the present to a future thousands of years away and to conceive of a relationship between time and eternity in which the fate of the world is inextricably bound up with happenings in the timeless realm. The basic characteristics of eternity are expressed in the world of time and are, in turn, dependent upon the world of time for their successful playing out. In this scheme, eternity needs time just as much as the world of time needs eternity, and we human beings participate in the work of eternity. Zoroastrianism introduced into the human race's long cultural conversation the idea of a cosmic purpose that moves all things toward a single end or goal. We human beings may take an active part in that movement, and as a result we may experience time as a meaningful journey toward greater life rather than a meaningless circle culminating in death. With Zarathustra, there came into the world a model by which humans could transcend the immediate moment and participate in the end and goal of all creation. With this philosophy, we could finally say that the world of time had a goal. It was a remarkable idea, and perhaps one of the few truly profound and revolutionary ideas in the history of human thought.

There is an optimism in this vision. If time is headed somewhere, then life becomes charged with ethical meaning, for individuals can align themselves with the forces of light or the forces of darkness and either hurry the process along or slow it down. By choosing an ethical life, human beings can actually participate in the work and purpose of the entire universe.

Augustine, influenced indirectly by Zoroastrianism, applied the idea to Christianity and provided believers with a vision of where time and the universe were headed. Augustine has been lurking in the background of this book almost from the beginning, for he was a man who took time very seriously. At the heart of his biography, *The Confessions*, lay the question of what time means. It was a question that obsessed him, for if time is the arena in which an individual life unfolds, then it is in the world of time that one must find meaning or not at all. So he asked some very modern questions. Is there a pattern to the life we lead, or is life just a random series of events that end in death? How does the hand of eternity work in the world of time?

Augustine was born in 354 C.E. in the Roman province of Numidia to a Christian mother and a pagan father. In his autobiography, written when he was about forty-five, we read of how this brilliant, classically educated man struggled to find a sense of meaning in his life at a time when the Roman empire was crumbling and the classical world was about to give way to a new world and new religion. As Donald Wilcox points out, "Augustine's curiosity about time was not a speculative whim but a deep personal need to understand the changes that had made him who he was."[4] In Augustine's view, time is primarily an activity of the human soul. It is part and parcel of being conscious. He used the word *attentio* to express the way the soul regards the passage of time through the present. We notice time by paying attention to change in the outer world. Eternity, for Augustine, was where we were headed. God's plan for the individual was to bring the soul gradually through the world

of time to eternity. Augustine saw this clearly in his own
life story.

But what of the universe? he asked. What of human history? What is its goal and direction? Is this great ship headed
anywhere at all? Augustine was pressed to address these questions by a specific historical cataclysm, a series of violent
attacks on the chief city of his time. In August 410, Rome
was sacked by Alaric and his Goth army. They had laid siege
to the city some two years before and had reduced the inhabitants to cannibalism, but this time they entered the city to
loot and burn, and the Romans were able to offer only con-
fused and inconsequential resistance. Rome had not been the
political capital of the empire since the emperor's move
to Ravenna some time before, but the sacking of the old capital was highly symbolic. Rome, the eternal city, had represented tranquillity, stability, order, and empire for the past
thousand years. If it fell, people realized, then who or what
could be safe?

Many Romans blamed the invasion on the fact that so
many people had turned away from the classical gods and had
embraced the new God of Christianity. Augustine, obviously,
could not take this challenge sitting down. For the next thirteen years, as political instability and war raged and as the old
Roman empire teetered on the edge of collapse, he wrote the
twenty-two books that would become *The City of God*, and in
the process he forged a vision of an entire universe tending
toward eternity.

By Augustine's time, some three hundred years had
elapsed since Jesus had left his followers behind with an admonition to wait for his second coming. While many Christians believed that the coming of Jesus was imminent, others
were trying to redefine just what Jesus might have meant by

"later." Origen and others had speculated about reincarnation and a final restoration of some kind that would embrace the whole universe.[5]

To Augustine, the Bible presented the history of the entire universe from beginning to end. The story from Genesis through Apocalypse chronicles the struggle between two major "cities," the City of God and the City of Man. In his *Confessions*, Augustine had already explored how the various strands of good and evil in one's own life could lead to eternity. Now he would attempt to prove that the history of the human race paralleled the experience of each individual. He would show that just as each person goes through a gradual process of enlightenment, so does all humanity.

With his Bible at hand, Augustine skillfully blended events from secular history with events from sacred history to show a grand pattern to it all. Beginning with the beginning, Augustine recapitulated all of history, both pagan and sacred, from the creation of the angels through the origin of evil, all the way through the Old Testament up through Jesus and onward to the final end of time and eternity beyond it. *The City of God* is breathtaking in its scope, and it bequeathed to the Western mind a sense of history as a single unified process, directed by the will of God toward a common end revealed in Scriptures. History was the movement of the whole universe toward eternity. In the end, time itself would cease to be, and all the righteous would be swept up into the eternal presence of God.

Out of Augustine's grand conception of history sprang the sense of progressive optimism that has characterized the Western mind for almost two thousand years. Augustine's articulation of a universal teleology entered forever into our discussion of the nature of time. Medieval historians believed that they were living in the final age before the second coming of Christ, which would be the end of time. The idea of history progressing through time toward a goal continued in the Renaissance, when our modern idea of "progress" was born. Even after the West became largely secular, the idea persisted. When, in the eighteenth century, the Marquis de Condorcet proposed the idea that history was progressing toward a perfect society, he was sowing seed in ground prepared by Augustine, simply substituting a perfect secular society for the heavenly city that Augustine saw at the end of time. Similarly, when Charles Lyell and other geologists in the late 1700s put forth their "evolutionary" schemes about the development of the earth, and when Charles Darwin came out with his theory of biological evolution in 1859, the West had been mentally prepared since Augustine to accept the idea that the universe progresses, or evolves, through time. Karl Marx, in his dialectical materialism, also imagined a grand pattern to historical time that would lead to the ideal society based on a dictatorship of the proletariat. In the United States, nineteenth-century progressives and capitalists made a virtual god out of progress.

But, as these examples show, by modern times progress was conceived of in essentially secular and material terms. The mechanism of historical progress remained, but the divine point of progress was lost. By the twentieth century, the mechanistic view of time had triumphed. Even though we understood more clearly than ever from a scientific point of view how the universe worked, we had given up belief in a spiritual end toward which it was headed. The result of the loss of a sacred dimension to time and history was the sense of time famine with which this book began. Our rushed lives seem devoid of any meaningful context. As in the old airplane joke, we are totally lost, but at least we are making good time.

As I've tried to show in this essay on finding sacred time, it is possible to live one's way back into a sense of sacred time on an individual basis. But is it also possible once again to achieve a shared vision of the end and direction of time of the sort that Zarathustra gave the ancient world and Augustine offered the Christian? I ask this in the midst of a world currently torn apart by sectarian wars in which true believers of various religions slaughter one another over competing visions of eternity, where a tenuous peace in the Middle East hinges on the partition of the holy city of Jerusalem. In a world threatened by religious fundamentalism of all kinds, is it not better to cling to the secular, mechanistic view of the world and time rather than risk more bloodshed? If so, then we are back to the beginning of this book. But if we are to reclaim a sense of sacred time, we must find a new way of understanding our world and its relation to eternity, a way that combines what we know from the advances of science with what we aspire to in our religious beliefs.

In the mid-twentieth century, a Christian thinker, Pierre Teilhard de Chardin, attempted to do just that, and his writings may offer us a model on which we can begin to build. Teilhard tried to synthesize modern science with the Augustinian Christian vision of time and history. In his many writings, most of which were suppressed until after his death in 1955, he attempted to fuse what he knew as a man of science with what he believed as a man of God. His sweeping vision is, I believe, the modern equivalent of the scope and majesty of Augustine's *City of God*.

As both a Catholic priest and a research scientist, Teilhard embodied the contradictions of the modern world. He was born in 1881, a mere twenty-two years after the publication of Darwin's *Origin of Species* ushered in the modern view of human evolutionary history. Ironically, the Vatican made Thomas Aquinas's medieval philosophy the official philosophy of the Catholic Church at roughly the same time. Entering the Society of Jesus at eighteen, Teilhard soon became interested in the biological sciences, and a reading of Henri Bergson convinced him of the truth of evolution. But how could he bridge the gulf between the cold mechanism of Darwinian theory that he learned in the sciences and his deeply felt intuition that the world was governed by a divine intelligence and was heading in the direction outlined by Augustine in *The City of God*? That the universe had within it a massive controlling intelligence or spirit was never a question for him. In *The Mass on the World*, published in 1964 but written in the early 1920s, Teilhard recounts a mystical experience he had in the desert, a moment when he felt, resonating in the core of his being, the living presence of God in all creation. Teilhard's description of the experience is positively Wordsworthian in its deeply felt intuition of a great mind rolling through all things. At the same time, however, his scientific education taught him to be skeptical of such emotional, unprovable experiences and ideas. He spent the rest of his life trying to articulate his deep conviction that science and religion, intelligence and intuition, were not contradictory but were complementary ways of knowing and participating in the universe.[6]

The near-mystical intuition permeating all of Teilhard's religious writing reached its fullest synthesis in *The Phenomenon of Man*. I first encountered this work when I was, for two years in the late sixties, a Jesuit novice. Even though Teilhard had died in 1955, his work was new to the world and still highly controversial. I remember how the eyes of the old Jesuit librarian at the novitiate grew round when I checked out the works of Teilhard one after the other. In the jargon of the day, they blew me away with their scope and vision and, most of all, with the sheer audacity of the enterprise Teilhard had set for himself. At the time I first read them, of course, I did not fully understand the implications of what I was reading (I may still not today), but I think I glimpsed the direction in which Teilhard was going, and I wanted to follow.

During my recent sabbatical year, as I found myself pondering questions of time's direction, I turned once again to Teilhard. Even after a quarter century of study and perspective, I am in no better position to evaluate his paleontology or anthropology, but today I appreciate much more the sheer poetic power of the man's vision, for what Teilhard holds out for us is a unified and optimistic vision of the future of individuals, the planet, and the universe itself, as well as the possibility of reconciling revealed truth with scientific fact.

In his master work, *The Phenomenon of Man*, Teilhard tried to synthesize the scientific enterprise of Western civilization with a religious vision of a cosmos filled with divine energy. In addition to the world of external appearances, which was governed by the mathematical laws of physics, Teilhard also believed in the existence of a world "within" things. It is, Teilhard said, outside of the ability of physics to measure or describe this world, since it is accessible only by "direct intuition." Synonyms for this "within" are consciousness and spontaneity which exist in some form in all matter but manifest themselves most fully in the human species, or at least we humans directly experience our own "within" in the form of our consciousness of the universe around us and of the universe within that we call the self.[7]

For Teilhard, the world of physical matter and the inner world of consciousness so thoroughly interpenetrate as to be inseparable. In a reversal of the traditional Platonic notion of the physical world being a mere model of a spiritual world of forms, Teilhard believed that the physical world actually brings forth the inner world of consciousness. Spirit, in a sense, depends on matter.

Teilhard rather poetically imagined the world as concentric spheres of increasing complexity. At the center of the earth lies the mineral core. Surrounding it is the stone mantle of the earth's crust and its solid surface on which rests the water layer of the oceans, lakes, and rivers. Then comes the layer of atmosphere and above that the stratosphere. This organization, of course, is reminiscent of the Great Chain of Being or of Ptolemaic astronomy with its neat organization of nesting spheres, but unlike the static worldview of the ancient astronomers, Teilhard conceived this world as dynamic. It is not an eternal organization established in a moment and unchanged since the beginning of time. Rather, creation is an ongoing and additive process, and each new stage has its roots in the previous stage. The world accumulates over time, and it has a tendency toward order rather than chaos. The oldest forms of physical matter formed themselves according to simple, stable, and geometric patterns like crystals. In Teilhard's view, this "crystalling world" seems to desire order. But no matter how orderly, a world composed of merely crystals is closed-ended and limited.

So the next level or stage of development arrived, and this he called the "polymerizing world." It is the highly complex world of organic compounds and it is open-ended and dynamic, its components constantly combining, growing, and developing into new forms. Here Teilhard parts ways with fundamentalists who say the world was created once and for all.

Over time nature "experiments" by way of genetic mutations, seeking opportunities for further growth and complexity. Through its experimentation, nature is trying on, as it were, various forms. However, Teilhard said, the process is not random, as Darwinians would believe. Rather, in Teilhard's view, the mutations of nature represent a sort of rudimentary consciousness within the world of matter that is seeking to evolve to more complex arrangements. Teilhard would say, then, that the whole universe, from its very beginning, desired consciousness, and so evolution conspired to evolve consciousness to as complex and highly developed a form as it could. Most of us would say that consciousness as such began with the human species, but Teilhard's view is more radical. According to him, it began hundreds of millions of years ago. He wrote, "we must assume psychic life to 'begin' in the world with the first appearance of organized life, in other words, the cell. . . . I assumed a decisive step in the progress of consciousness on earth to have taken place at this particular stage of evolution."[8]

The so-called Darwinian accidents of genetic mutation, then, really represented the attempts of a dynamic universal consciousness to bring itself to fuller expression. This tendency toward consciousness runs through all of creation and is profuse and ingenious, abundantly creative. Where seeds appear, they appear by the millions, and any one of them may contain the germ of a new experiment by nature to expand its consciousness. Conditioned by what is possible within its environment, life's profusion gropes for new solutions. By the fact of the sheer numbers of organisms, this groping is "pervading everything so as to try everything, and trying everything so as to find everything."[9] Having billions of years at its disposal, nature has the capacity to run all possible permutations on this thing called life. Beneath nature's rich abundance and manifold diversity, therefore, Teilhard saw a single, unified process, the work of a single intelligence seeking to become conscious of itself. "Taken in its totality," he wrote, "the living substance spread over the earth—from the very first stages of its evolution—traces the lineaments of one single and gigantic organism."[10]

Looking at the development of higher life forms, Teilhard saw the emergence of insects, reptiles, mammals, primates, and then humans as one long march toward increasingly complex consciousness. The nervous systems of animals developed over time toward more complex and deeper "interiority," and we can classify creatures by their degree of "cerebralization." Teilhard would say that in the history of evolution there has never been development toward lesser consciousness. Rather, one can see only a continual rise in consciousness. Consciousness was prepared for in inorganic nature, and it finally came to manifest itself in a unique way in the human animal's self-conscious reflection.

According to Teilhard, the focus of further evolution will not be in the direction of further physical change but of spiritual change. Nature's drive toward further self-consciousness will cease being in human biological evolution and instead will become internal, nonphysical, focused on the "within" of things as this universal consciousness brings us, and thus itself, toward a fuller, more complex realization.

In human beings, this cosmic consciousness achieved the ability to turn inward and observe itself. It became self-reflective. We humans are capable not only of knowing but of knowing that we know. This represents yet a further "ascent of consciousness," a qualitative leap forward from the kind of consciousness possessed by our primate ancestors and cousins.[11] In us, further development of consciousness can take place without much physiological change. Further progress will come through education and thought, and it will be primarily cultural and psychological rather than physical. Teilhard called this process the "hominization" of humankind, our coming as a species into fuller consciousness of ourselves and our universe.

This is tantamount to the development of a new and larger sphere of creation, what Teilhard called the "noosphere." The noosphere, the sphere of thought or consciousness, encompasses all the other spheres of the world and extends out to the farthest reaches of human understanding. It forms a "thinking layer" that has spread over the earth with our species and that now, thanks to telecommunications and the Internet, blankets the globe with an interchange of thoughts and ideas to a density perhaps unimaginable even to Teilhard. With the emergence of the noosphere, writes Teilhard, the earth "gets a new skin. Better still it finds its soul."[12]

Teilhard saw the current age as one of radical transformation. A modern person, with a worldview based on dynamic, open-ended systems in which everything develops, expands, and moves outward, would find the pre-Copernican world suffocating with its nesting crystalline spheres each in its place, moving forever in an unchanging round. The exploding universe with its endlessly unfolding consciousness is a new cosmos, a mental world in which our species has not tried to live before.

One of the main trends of twentieth-century philosophy and literature has been to see the situation of modern humankind as an absurdity. The main stance of such modernist writers as Jean-Paul Sartre, Samuel Beckett, Eugene Ionesco, and Albert Camus has been anxiety in the face of a universal void, futility in confronting an absurd universe, feelings of insignificance before a new cosmos, vaster and much older than any we've dealt with before. The modernist view is grim.

If, however, we choose to see human beings as the consciousness of a being whose purpose and meaning lie in its own unfolding, then we can choose to participate in that universal unfolding of consciousness "till we arrive . . . At the utmost limits of ourselves."[13] And since consciousness in this sense has no limit, then the endpoint is infinity. Teilhard believed that, as a species, we can be satisfied with nothing less.

Nature, the whole history of evolution, apparently conspired for countless millennia to bring human consciousness forth; therefore, we should have faith, hope, and confidence to press the development of consciousness forward even further. The very roundness of the earth, says Teilhard, forces coalescence and assures connectedness. We cannot help coming around upon ourselves again. In the end, the roundness of the universe itself may lead to a "mega-synthesis" of "ever more complexity and thus ever more consciousness."[14]

For Teilhard, of course, the omega point of total convergence and total consciousness was Christ himself. As God become human, Christ, for the Christian, is the timeless creative principle within the finite world of time. What Augustine saw as the end of time in the second coming of Christ Teilhard saw as the culmination of millions of years of coming to full and cosmic consciousness. Christ as beginning and end, as alpha and omega, will be the point at which all our individualities merge and fuse at the highest level of consciousness.

In a world torn by sectarian strife, we may wish to step back further from Teilhard and see *all* the world's religious traditions as attempts to articulate, in various languages, the human race's evolving consciousness of itself and the universe. The panoply of the world's religions, the many avenues we as a species have explored to enter sacred time, are all part of the universe's own drive to make itself fully conscious.

The transcendent energy that makes all this growth toward consciousness possible, says Teilhard, is love. Love is an energy that, like consciousness, is built into the very fabric of the universe. Love is the name we give to the power in elements and in species that allows them to combine, change, and grow. Love seems like an odd word to come from a man calling himself a scientist, yet by it he means the subtle power by which we decenter ourselves and change and grow into something as yet unimagined. "Love alone is capable of uniting living beings in such a way as to complete and fulfill them, for it alone takes them and joins them by what is deepest in themselves."[15]

Is love, then, the end of time? Is that the purpose and the goal toward which the universe has been tending? Is that where it all ought to end? The idea seems at once inadequate and also overwhelming. And yet it seems to me that the wisdom books of the world's great religious traditions tell us exactly that. According to the biblical formula, "God is love and he who abides in love abides in God and God in him." The more we partake of love, the more we partake of the infinite; that, it seems, is the end, or goal, of time. For the phrase "the end of time" has a double sense. An end is a terminal point, a destination, and as such we are never quite there. We are always arriving, never quite arrived.

So what is the point? Is this vast show going anywhere in particular, or is the whole universe just a large mechanism unwinding itself indefinitely into the future? Will there be an end to time, a time when time itself will be no more, when the stately procession of heavenly bodies across the canopy of the sky will finally halt? Will time end in darkness or in light?

But in another way, "the end of time" is with us here and now, for the other meaning of "end" is a goal or purpose, the end that draws us forward from the present into the future. In that sense, we live daily with the end of time, for our constant purpose is to expand the consciousness of ourselves and in the process to expand the consciousness of the universe itself through compassion and love.

This, then, may be what passes for faith in the contemporary world. It is not faith in any particular god or creed, though that may be important to many. Rather, it is the profession of the larger faith in which those faiths exist: the belief that the universe is not a cold mechanism into we have been thrust, but it is our home to understand and become conscious of. Ultimately, faith is the irrational leap into the belief that the universe does make sense, unprovable though that assumption is turning out to be. This is the faith we invigorate when we search for sacred time, and this is why sacred time must be found. Finding sacred time, maintaining our connection with it, we may have the leisure to lie back and look at the stars and say yes, the end of time is now and forever.

Notes

CHAPTER 1. *No Time Like the Present*

1. Martin Heidegger, *Being and Time*, trans. John Macquarrie and Edward Robinson (New York: Harper and Row, 1962).
2. Ussher fixed the exact time as "the first part of the night which preceded the 23rd of October in the year of the Julian period 710," or about 3963 B.C.E. Cf. Donald J. Wilcox, *The Measure of Times Past: Pre-Newtonian Chronologies and the Rhetoric of Relative Time* (Chicago: University of Chicago Press, 1987), 187.
3. In *The Descent of Man*, Darwin noted that the evolution of humans was so gradual as to make impossible any exact dating of when "man" as a distinct species occurred, but he knew from Lyell and Thompson that geologic time stretched back millions of years, and he believed with the uniformitarians that evolutionary changes were slow and gradual. Clearly the date of the origin of humankind had to be pushed back very much farther than anyone had thought before.
4. Edward T. Hall, *The Dance of Life: The Other Dimension of Time* (Garden City, N.J.: Anchor Doubleday, 1983).
5. Karen Horney, *The Neurotic Personality of Our Time* (New York: Norton, 1937), 34.
6. Gary Eberle, *The Geography of Nowhere: Finding One's Self in the Postmodern World* (Kansas City: Sheed and Ward, 1994), 13–17.
7. Reinhart Koselleck, *Futures Past: On the Semantics of Historical Time*, trans. Keith Tribe (Cambridge: MIT Press, 1985), xxiv.
8. "Golem," in *Encyclopaedia Judaica*, ed. Geoffery Wigoder (Jerusalem: Encyclopaedia Judaica, 1994).

CHAPTER 2. *A Sense of Timing*

1. G. J. Whitrow, *Time in History: Views of Time from Prehistory to the Present Day* (Oxford: Oxford University Press, 1989), 18.

2. Josef Pieper, *Leisure, the Basis of Culture,* trans. Alexander Dru (New York: Pantheon, 1964), 35.

3. Tracy Kidder, *The Soul of a New Machine* (Boston: Little Brown, 1981).

4. Edward T. Hall, *The Dance of Life: The Other Dimension of Time* (Garden City, N.J.: Anchor Doubleday, 1983), 21.

CHAPTER 3. *Time and Eternity*

1. Augustine of Hippo, *The Confessions of St. Augustine,* ed. J. M. Lelen (New York: Catholic Book Publishing, 1952), 293.

2. Augustine's treatment of time is addressed more fully in the afterword.

3. Edward T. Hall, *The Dance of Life: The Other Dimension of Time* (Garden City, N.J.: Anchor Doubleday, 1983), 161.

4. Ibid., 118.

5. The story of this research through the mid-1980s is told in Martin C. Moore-Ede and Frank M. Sulzman and Charles A. Fuller, *The Clocks that Time Us: Physiology of the Circadian Timing System* (Cambridge, Mass.: Harvard University Press, 1982).

6. Eugene D. D'Aquili, "Myth, Ritual and the Archetypal Hypothesis," *Zygon* 21: 2 (June 1986), 158.

7. For an excellent and detailed technical discussion of the neurophysiological structures involved, see Eugene D'Aquili and Andrew B. Newberg, "Religious and Mystical States: A Neuropsychological Model," *Zygon* 28:2 (June 1993), 177–200.

8. Jean Guitton, *Man in Time,* trans. Adrienne Foulke (Notre Dame, Ind.: University of Notre Dame Press, 1966), 28.

9. Charles D. Laughlin, "The Ritual Transformation of Experience," *Studies in Symbolic Interaction* 7: A (1986), 113.

10. Ibid., 114.

11. Ibid., 110.

12. Hall, *Dance,* 135–36.

13. Ibid., 161.

14. Klaus Fink, "The Bi-Logic Perception of Time," *International Journal of Psychoanalysis* 74:2 (April 1993), 303.

15. Ibid.

16. Marie-Louise von Franz, "Time and Synchronicity in Analytic Psy-

chology," in *The Voices of Time: A Cooperative Survey of Man's Views of Time as Expressed by the Sciences and Humanities*, ed. J. T. Fraser (Amherst: University of Massachusetts Press, 1981), 221.

CHAPTER 4. *Books of Hours*

1. This discussion of the history of monasticism is summarized from John Daly Lowrie, *Benedictine Monasticism: Its Formation and Development Through the 12th Century* (New York: Sheed and Ward, 1965).

2. After the invention of the clock, None got moved up three hours to become our noon, a time of midday prayer.

3. Ricardo Quiñones, *The Renaissance Discovery of Time* (Cambridge: Harvard University Press, 1972), 7.

4. James J. Rorimer, *The Hours of Jeanne D'Evreux* (New York: Metropolitan Museum of Art, 1957), 7.

5. The Limbourg brothers seem to have stopped their work in 1416, and Colombe resumed it in 1485.

6. An excellent facsimile with commentary is available. Cf. Raymond Cazelles and Johannes Rathofer, *Illuminations of Heaven and Earth: The Très Riches Heures du Duc de Berry* (New York: Harry N. Abrams, 1988). The illustrations of the months are widely available on the Internet.

7. Every château needs its dragon, and every dragon has its legend. This particular one concerns Melusine, daughter of a fairy, who was human in form most of the week but whose legs turned into those of a dragon every Saturday. She made her husband, Count Raymondin, swear he would never look at her on that day, but one Saturday, inevitably, he came upon her bathing and saw her dragon legs. Surprised, she turned into a full dragon and flew out the window. Now she acts as a guardian to the castle, crying out when bad fortune is about to come upon the house. She also represents the fertility of the land. Dragons in European literature generally guard a treasure hoard, but this female dragon seems more like the sky dragons of Chinese mythology, bringers of spring rain and new crops.

8. Harry Bober, "The Zodiacal Miniature of the Très Riches Heures of the Duke of Berry," *Journal of the Warburg and Courtauld Institutes* 2 (1948), 12.

9. *Clocca* is the Latin word for bell from which derives the English word clock. Bell is *Glock* in German, *cloche* in French.

10. Eviatar Zerubavel, *Hidden Rhythms: Schedules and Calendars in Social Life* (Chicago: University of Chicago Press, 1981), 41.

11. Translation by Marianne Graff.

CHAPTER 5. *The Triumph of the Clock*

1. Carlo M. Cipolla, *Clocks and Culture: 1300–1700* (New York: Norton, 1978), 40–41.

2. Ibid.

3. Ibid., *165*.

4. Daniel Boorstin, *The Discoverers* (New York: Random House, 1983), 40.

5. Lewis Mumford, *Technics and Civilization* (New York: Harbinger, 1963), 14.

6. Ricardo Quiñones, *The Renaissance Discovery of Time* (Cambridge: Harvard University Press, 1972), 13.

7. Donald J. Wilcox, *The Measure of Times Past: Pre-Newtonian Chronologies and the Rhetoric of Relative Time* (Chicago: University of Chicago Press, 1987), 163.

8. In Quiñones, *Renaissance*, 72.

9. Ibid., x.

10. Ibid., 327.

11. William Shakespeare, *Richard II*, 5.5.49–50, in *The Norton Shakespeare*, ed. Stephen Greenblatt (New York: Norton, 1997).

12. Ben Jonson, "Love Freed from Ignorance and Folly," in *Ben Jonson, Volume 7*, ed. C. H. Herford Percy and Evelyn Simpson (Oxford: Clarendon, 1941), lines 363–64.

13. In Perry Miller, *The New England Mind* (Cambridge: Harvard University Press, 1954), 44.

14. In Gary Cross, *A Social History of Leisure Since 1600* (State College, Pa.: Venture Publishing, 1990), 28.

15. In Eviatar Zerubavel, *Hidden Rhythms: Schedules and Calendars in Social Life* (Chicago: University of Chicago Press, 1981), 55.

16. In Boorstin, *The Discoverers*, 71.

17. In Marie Boas Hall, *Robert Boyle on Natural Philosophy* (Bloomington: Indiana University Press, 1965), 146.

18. Cipolla, *Clocks*, 105.

19. G. J. Whitrow, *Time in History: Views of Time from Prehistory to the Present Day* (Oxford: Oxford University Press, 1989), 137.

20. Cipolla, *Clocks*, 75. Not everyone was impressed with the European way of thinking about and measuring time. Some years ago, National Public Radio broadcast a report about a Native American in upstate New Hampshire who was working on a dictionary of his people's almost lost language. Its only existing dictionary was compiled by French Jesuit missionaries who came to convert the natives in the seventeenth century. The language had many peculiarities, especially when it came to naming things imported by Europeans. The word they developed for clock, for example, was a long one, consisting of a root, many prefixes, and a suffix or two, which translated as "the thing that makes noise for no reason." At Fort Michilimackinac in Mackinaw City, Michigan, a reconstructed eighteenth-century fort includes a chapel where an antique clock is prominently displayed as it was in colonial times. Records at the fort indicate that the natives who came to the chapel thought the clock was some kind of holy object, perhaps even a god, because of the frequency with which the Europeans consulted it. Perhaps they were not far off the mark.

21. Mumford, *Technics*, 42.

22. Cipolla, *Clocks*, 69.

23. Boorstin, *The Discoverers*, 51.

24. For more complete technical details on Harrison's invention and subsequent clock makers, refer to R. T. Gould, *John Harrison and His Timekeepers* (London: National Maritime Museum, 1958).

25. Charles, Dickens. *Dombey and Son.* (Oxford: Oxford University Press, 1996), 185.

26. Henry David Thoreau. *The Portable Thoreau*, ed. Carl Bode. (New York: Viking, 1964), 368–369.

27. Mumford, 269.

28. J. T. Fraser, ed., *The Voices of Time: A Cooperative Survey of Man's Views of Time as Expressed by the Sciences and Humanities* (Amherst: University of Massachusetts Press, 1981), 387.

CHAPTER 6. *In Search of Sacred Time*

1. E.E. Evans Pritchard, *Theories of Primitive Religion* (Oxford: Clarendon, 1965), 15.
2. Emil Durkheim, *The Elementary Forms* (New York: The Free Press, 1965), 53–54.
3. Ibid., 56.
4. In using the word "ritual" here, I want to include also those psychological states achieved through contemplation or meditation or prayer.
5. Cf. Josef Pieper, *In Tune with the World: A Theory of Festivity,* trans. Richard and Clara Winston (New York: Harcourt, Brace and World, Inc., 1965), 6.
6. Ibid., 7.
7. Josef Pieper, *Leisure, the Basis of Culture,* trans. Alexander Dru (New York: Pantheon Books, 1964), 38.
8. Tamara Hareven, *Family Time and Industrial Time* (Cambridge: Cambridge University Press, 1982)
9. Hugh Cunningham, *Leisure in the Industrial Revolution* (New York: St. Martin's, 1980), 45.
10. Pieper, *In Tune,* 15.
11. Ibid., 10, (emphasis his).
12. Pieper, *Leisure,* 48.
13. Ibid., 28.
14. Passages cited from Pieper's work *passim.*
15. Pieper, *Leisure,* 31.
16. Cf. G. J. Whitrow, *Time in History: Views of Time from Prehistory to the Present Day* (Oxford: Oxford University Press, 1989), 109.
17. Pieper, *Leisure,* 49.
18. Pieper, *In Tune,* 23, (emphasis his).
19. Pieper, *In Tune,* 29.
20. Ibid., 46.
21. Joost A. M. Merloo, "The Time Sense in Psychiatry," *The Voices of Time: A Cooperative Survey of Man's Views of Time as Expressed by the Sciences and Humanities,* ed. J. T. Fraser (Amherst: University of Massachusetts Press, 1981), 250.

CHAPTER 7. *Finding Sacred Time*

1. Abraham Joshua Heschel, *The Sabbath: Its Meaning for Modern Man* (New York: Farrar, Strauss and Young, 1951), 22–23.

2. Phillip Sigal, *Judaism: The Evolution of a Faith* (Grand Rapids, Mich.: Eerdmans, 1988), 251.

3. Eviatar Zerubavel, *Hidden Rhythms: Schedules and Calendars in Social Life* (Chicago: University of Chicago Press, 1981), 117.

4. Ibid., 131.

5. Ibid., 128–129.

6. Heschel, *Sabbath*, 101.

7. The Celtic Christian year also began as the season darkened, on Samhain, All Hallows' Eve. The Irish year was explicitly tied to the agricultural cycle, and was divided into quarters, the passage to each new quarter being marked by so-called great days. St. Brigid's Day was celebrated on February 1, May Day on May 1, and Doon Sunday or Lamas Day on August 1. In the midst of each quarter, or season, another high day was marked. In winter, Christmas fell halfway between All Hallows' and St. Brigid's Day. In Spring St. Patrick's Day fell halfway between St. Brigid's feast and May Day. In June came St. John's or Midsummer Eve. And thus the seasonal cycle rolled on, beginning in the darkness of winter and ending with the rich harvest of autumn. Henry Glassie, *All Silver and No Brass* (Bloomington: University of Indiana Press, 1975).

8. Christmas was set at December 25 by the early church in order to displace the pagan feast of Saturnalia.

9. Eamon Duffy, *The Stripping of the Altars: Traditional Religion in England 1400–1580* (New Haven: Yale University Press, 1992), 22.

10. Jean Guitton, *Man in Time*, trans. Adrienne Foulke (Notre Dame, Ind.: University of Notre Dame Press, 1966), 83.

11. Josef Pieper, *In Tune with the World: A Theory of Festivity*, trans. Richard and Clara Winston (New York: Harcourt, Brace, and World, 1965), 27.

12. Guitton, *Man in Time*, 37.

AFTERWORD: *The End of Time*

1. Oddly enough, this belief is also encountered in Plato's *Statesman*.
2. Cf. Joseph Campbell, *Occidental Mythology*, Volume 3 of *The Masks of God* (New York: Penguin, 1964), 189 ff.; Richard Cavendish, ed., *An Illustrated Encyclopedia of Mythology* (London: Orbis, 1980), 40 ff.; G. J. Whitrow, *Time in History: Views of Time from Prehistory to the Present Day* (Oxford: Oxford University Press, 1989), 35.
3. Campbell, *Occidental Mythology*, 200.
4. Donald J. Wilcox, *The Measure of Times Past: Pre-Newtonian Chronologies and the Rhetoric of Relative Time* (Chicago: University of Chicago Press, 1987), 120.
5. Eugene Portalie, *A Guide to the Thought of St. Augustine* (Chicago: Henry Regnery, 1960), 289.
6. Unfortunately, the church did not actively encourage this way of thought at that time. In 1926, his superiors dismissed him from the Institut Catholique in Paris where he had been trying to convince the church it should embrace the Darwinian point of view. He spent the next twenty years in China, where his paleontological work led to the discovery of Peking man and added scientific validation to his conviction that Darwin was correct. Although he could publish his scientific works, the church would not let him print his fascinating speculations about the religious dimensions of evolution. Teilhard was thus deprived of the public discussion and criticism that could have helped him further refine his thought. In private letters and discussions, however, he moved his thought forward in such works as *The Divine Milieu* and *The Phenomenon of Man* which were published posthumously and were translated into English only in the late 1950s and early 1960s.
7. In this, Teilhard was in line with the Catholic Church's teaching of nonoverlapping magisteria, that is, the idea that revealed truth and scientific fact are not in competition with each other but rather deal with separate areas of human experience. Science deals with physical realities, theology with spiritual ones. Pius XII, in *Humani Generis* (1950) had stated clearly that what science revealed about human evolution could be believed simultaneously with the church's teachings on Creation. For an excellent summary of this position, see Stephen Jay

Gould, "Nonoverlapping Magisteria," *Natural History*, 3 (1997), 16 ff.

8. Pierre Teilhard de Chardin, *The Phenomenon of Man*, trans. Bernard Wall (New York: Harper and Brothers, 1959), 88.

9. Ibid., 110.

10. Ibid., 112. The same idea would be articulated in the mid-1980s by James Lovelock when he put forth his Gaia hypothesis, the idea that the earth, taken as a whole, is an intelligent, self-regulating organism.

11. Ibid., 166.

12. Ibid., 182.

13. Ibid., 230.

14. Ibid., 244.

15. Ibid., 265.

Selected Bibliography

Abrams, Myer, et al. *The Norton Anthology of English Literature*. Volume 1, 6th edition. New York: Norton, 1993.

Alexander, J. J. G. *The Master of Mary of Burgundy: A Book of Hours for Engelbert of Nassau*. New York: George Braziller, 1970.

Aristotle. *Aristotle's Physics, Books III and IV*. Trans. Edward Hussey. New York: Oxford University Press, 1983.

Augustine of Hippo. *The City of God*. Trans. Marcus Dods. New York: Modern Library, 1960.

———. *The Confessions of St. Augustine*. Ed. J. M. Lelen. New York: Catholic Book Publishing, 1952.

Barr, James. *Biblical Words for Time*. London: SCM Press, 1962.

Beckett, Wendy. *The Duke and the Peasant: Life in the Middle Ages: The Calendar Pictures in the Duc de Berry's Très Riches Heures*. New York: Prestel, 1997.

Bender, John, and David E. Wellbury. *Chronotypes: The Construction of Time*. Stanford, Calif.: Stanford University Press, 1991.

Bober, Harry. "The Zodiacal Miniature of the Très Riches Heures of the Duke of Berry." *Journal of the Warburg and Courtauld Institutes* 2 (1948).

Boorstin, Daniel. *The Discoverers*. New York: Random House, 1983.

Campbell, Joseph. *Occidental Mythology*. Volume 3 of *The Masks of God*. New York: Penguin, 1964.

———. *The Way of the Animal Powers*. San Francisco: Harper and Row, 1983.

Cary-Elwes, C., and C. Wybroune. *Work and Prayer: The Rule of St. Benedict for Lay People*. CD-ROM Medieval Realms. London: Burns & Oates, The British Library, 1992.

Cavendish, Richard, ed. *An Illustrated Encyclopedia of Mythology*. London: Orbis, 1980.

Cazelles, Raymond, and Johannes Rathofer. *Illuminations of Heaven and*

Earth: The Très Riches Heures du Duc de Berry. New York: Harry N. Abrams, 1988.

Chaucer, Geoffrey. *The Complete Poetry and Prose of Geoffrey Chaucer*. Ed. John Fisher. New York: Holt, Rinehart and Winston, 1977.

Cipolla, Carlo M. *Clocks and Culture: 1300–1700*. New York: Norton, 1978.

Cloudsley-Thompson, J. L. "Time Sense of Animals." In *The Voices of Time: A Cooperative Survey of Man's Views of Time as Expressed by the Sciences and Humanities*. Ed. J. T. Fraser. Amherst: University of Massachusetts Press, 1981.

Cohen, John. "Subjective Time." In *The Voices of Time: A Cooperative Survey of Man's Views of Time as Expressed by the Sciences and Humanities*. Ed. J. T. Fraser. Amherst: University of Massachusetts Press, 1981.

Corben, Henry, et al. *Man and Time: Papers from the Eranos Yearbooks*. Bollingen Series XXX. New York: Pantheon, 1957.

Cross, Gary. *A Social History of Leisure Since 1600*. State College, Pa.: Venture Publishing, 1990.

Csikszentmihalyi, Mihaly. *Flow: The Psychology of Optimal Experience*. New York: HarperCollins, 1991.

Cunningham, Hugh. *Leisure in the Industrial Revolution*. New York: St. Martin's, 1980.

Daly, Lowrie John. *Benedictine Monasticism: Its Formation and Development Through the 12th Century*. New York: Sheed and Ward, 1965.

D'Aquili, Eugene D. "Myth, Ritual and the Archetypal Hypothesis." *Zygon* 21 (June 1986), 141–60.

D'Aquili, Eugene D., and Andrew B. Newberg. "Religious and Mystical States: A Neuropsychological Model." *Zygon* 28:2, (June 1993), 177–200.

Darwin, Charles. *The Origin of Species by Means of Natural Selection*. New York: Penguin, 1985.

Defoe, Daniel. *Robinson Crusoe and Journal of the Plague Year*. New York: Modern Library, 1948.

Delatte, Dom Paul. *A Commentary on The Rule of St. Benedict*. Trans. Dom Justin McCann. London: Burnes & Oates, 1921.

Dickens, Charles. *Dombey and Son*. Oxford: Oxford University Press, 1996.

———. *Hard Times for These Times*. New York: Penguin, 1995.

Dobzhansky, Theodosius. *The Biology of Ultimate Concern*. New York: New American Library, 1967.

Dubos, Rene. *Celebrations of Life*. New York: McGraw-Hill, 1981.

Duffy, Eamon. *The Stripping of the Altars: Traditional Religion in England 1400–1580*. New Haven: Yale University Press, 1992.

Durkheim, Emil. *The Elementary Forms*. New York: Free Press, 1965.

Eberle, Gary. *The Geography of Nowhere: Finding One's Self in the Postmodern World*. Kansas City: Sheed and Ward, 1994.

——. "The Ayenbite of Inwit." *Parabola* (Fall 1997), 66–70.

Eliade, Mircea. *Cosmos and History: The Myth of the Eternal Return*. New York: Harper Torchbooks, 1959.

Evans-Pritchard, E. E. *The Nuer*. Oxford: Clarendon, 1940.

——. *Theories of Primitive Religion*. Oxford: Clarendon, 1965.

Fink, Klaus. "The Bi-Logic Perception of Time." *International Journal of Psychoanalysis* 74:2 (April 1993), 303–12.

Foucault, Michel. *The Order of Things: An Archeology of the Human Sciences*. New York: Vintage, 1973.

Fraser, J. T., ed. *The Voices of Time: A Cooperative Survey of Man's Views of Time as Expressed by the Sciences and Humanities*. Amherst: University of Massachusetts Press, 1981.

Gardner, John, and John Maier, trans. *Gilgamesh*. New York: Vintage, 1985.

Glassie, Henry. *All Silver and No Brass*. Bloomington: University of Indiana Press, 1975.

Gleick, James. "Watch This Space." *The New York Times Magazine* 9 (July 1995), 14.

Gould, R. T. *John Harrison and His Timekeepers*. London: National Maritime Museum, 1958.

Gould, Stephen Jay. "Nonoverlapping Magisteria." *Natural Science* 3 (1997), 16.

Guitton, Jean. *Man in Time*. Trans. Adrienne Foulke. Notre Dame, Ind.: University of Notre Dame Press, 1966.

Hall, Edward T. *The Dance of Life: The Other Dimension of Time*. Garden City, N.J.: Anchor Doubleday, 1983.

Hall, Marie Boas. *Robert Boyle on Natural Philosophy*. Bloomington: Indiana University Press, 1965.

Hamilton, Edith. *Mythology: Timeless Tales of Gods and Heroes.* New York: Mentor, 1940.

Hareven, Tamara K. *Family Time and Industrial Time.* Cambridge: Cambridge University Press, 1982.

Harvey, David. *The Condition of Postmodernism: An Enquiry into the Origin of Cultural Change.* Cambridge: Blackwell, 1990.

Heidegger, Martin. *Being and Time.* Trans. John Macquarrie and Edward Robinson. New York: Harper and Row, 1962.

Heschel, Abraham Joshua. *The Sabbath: Its Meaning for Modern Man.* New York: Farrar, Straus and Young, 1951.

Hesiod. *Works and Days and Theogony.* Trans. Stanley Lombardo. Indianapolis: Hackett, 1993.

Horney, Karen. *The Neurotic Personality of Our Time.* New York: Norton, 1937.

Jonson, Ben. *Ben Jonson. Volume 7.* Ed. C. H. Herford Percy and Evelyn Simpson. Oxford: Clarendon, 1941.

Jung, Carl. *Aion: Researches into the Phenomenology of the Self. The Collected Works of C. G. Jung,* vol. 9, part 2. Trans. R. F. C. Hull. Princeton: Princeton University Press, 1978.

Kidder, Tracy. *The Soul of a New Machine.* Boston: Little Brown, 1981.

King, Ursula. *Towards a New Mysticism: Teilhard de Chardin and Eastern Religions.* New York: Seabury Press, 1980.

Koselleck, Reinhart. *Futures Past: On the Semantics of Historical Time.* Trans. Keith Tribe. Cambridge: MIT Press, 1985.

Laughlin, Charles D. "The Ritual Transformation of Experience." *Studies in Symbolic Interaction* 7:A (1986), 107–36.

Linder, Steffan. *The Harried Leisure Class.* New York: Columbia University Press, 1970.

Lurker, Manfred. *The Gods and Symbols of Ancient Egypt.* London: Thames and Hudson, 1980.

MacLean, P. D. *The Triune Concept of Brain and Behavior.* Ed. T. J. Boag and D. Campbell. Toronto: University of Toronto Press, 1973.

Marschack, Alexander. *The Roots of Civilization: The Cognitive Beginnings of Man's First Art, Symbol and Notation.* Mt. Kisco, N.Y.: Moyer Bell, 1991.

Merloo, Joost A. M. "The Time Sense in Psychiatry." In *The Voices of Time:*

A Cooperative Survey of Man's Views of Time as Expressed by the Sciences and Humanities. Ed. J. T. Fraser. Amherst: University of Massachusetts Press, 1981.

Miller, Perry. *The New England Mind.* Cambridge: Harvard University Press, 1954.

Moore, Wilbert. *Man, Time and Society.* New York: Wiley, 1963.

Moore-Ede, Martin C., and Frank M. Sulzman and Charles A. Fuller. *The Clocks That Time Us: Physiology of the Circadian Timing System.* Cambridge: Harvard University Press, 1982.

Mumford, Lewis. *Technics and Civilization.* New York: Harbinger, 1963.

Nakamura, Hajime. "Time In Indian and Japanese Thought." In *The Voices of Time: A Cooperative Survey of Man's Views of Time as Expressed by the Sciences and Humanities.* Ed. J. T. Fraser. Amherst: University of Massachusetts Press. 1981.

Newton, Isaac. *Sir Isaac Newton's Mathematical Principles of Natural Philosophy and His System of the World.* Trans. Florian Cajori. New York: Greenwood Press, 1962.

Pieper, Josef. *Leisure, the Basis of Culture.* Trans. Alexander Dru. New York: Pantheon, 1964.

——. *In Tune with the World: A Theory of Festivity.* Trans. Richard and Clara Winston. New York: Harcourt, Brace and World, 1965.

Plato. *The Dialogues of Plato.* Trans. Benjamin Jowett. New York: Random House, 1937.

——. *Plato's Timaeus.* Trans. Francis M. Cornford. New York: Liberal Arts Press, 1959.

Plotinus. *The Enneads.* Trans. Stephen MacKenna. London: Faber and Faber, 1962.

Portalie, Eugene. *A Guide to the Thought of St. Augustine.* Chicago: Henry Regnery, 1960.

Quiñones, Ricardo. *The Renaissance Discovery of Time.* Cambridge: Harvard University Press, 1972.

Rifkin, Jeremy. *Time Wars: The Primary Conflict in Human History.* New York: Henry Holt, 1987.

Rorimer, James J. *The Hours of Jeanne D'Evreux.* New York: Metropolitan Museum of Art, 1957.

Russel, J. L. "Time in Christian Thought." In *The Voices of Time: A Cooperative Survey of Man's Views of Time as Expressed by the Sciences and Humanities.*

Ed. J. T. Fraser. Amherst: University of Massachusetts Press, 1981.

Rybczynski, Witold. *Waiting for the Weekend*. New York: Pegasus, 1991.

Sato, Giei, and Eshin Nishimura. *Unsui: A Diary of Zen Monastic Life.* Honolulu: University of Hawaii Press, 1973.

Schor, Juliet B. *The Overworked American: The Unexpected Decline of Leisure.* New York: Basic Books, 1991.

Shakespeare, William. *The Norton Shakespeare*. Ed. Stephen Greenblatt. New York: Norton, 1997.

Siffre, Michel. *Beyond Time*. New York: McGraw-Hill, 1964.

Sigal, Phillip. *Judaism: The Evolution of a Faith*. Grand Rapids, Mich.: Eerdmans, 1988.

Simmel, Georg. "The Metropolis and Mental Life." In *The Sociology of Georg Simmel*. New York: Free Press, 1950.

Singer, Isaac Bashevis. *The Golem*. New York: Farrar, Straus and Giroux, 1996.

Smith, Warren Thomas. *Augustine: His Life and Thought*. Atlanta: John Knox, 1979.

Sorabji, Richard. *Time, Creation and the Continuum: Theories in Antiquity and the Early Middle Ages*. Ithaca, N.Y.: Cornell University Press, 1983.

Sterne, Laurence. *Tristram Shandy*. New York: Modern Library, n.d.

Teilhard de Chardin, Pierre. *The Divine Milieu: An Essay on the Interior Life.* Ed. Bernard Wall. New York: Harper and Brothers, 1960.

——. *Human Energy*. Trans. J. M. Cohen. New York: Harcourt Brace Jovanovitch, 1969.

——. *The Phenomenon of Man*. Trans. Bernard Wall. New York: Harper and Brothers, 1959.

Thoreau, Henry David. *The Portable Thoreau*. Ed. Carl Bode. New York: Viking, 1964.

Thucydides. *Thucydides*. Trans. Charles Foster Smith. Cambridge: Harvard University Press, 1912.

Toulson, Shirley. *The Celtic Year*. Rockport, Mass.: Element, 1993.

Les Très Riches Heures: The Medieval Seasons. New York: George Braziller, 1995.

Von Franz, Marie-Louise. "Time and Synchronicity in Analytic Psychology." In *The Voices of Time: A Cooperative Survey of Man's Views of Time as Expressed by the Sciences and Humanities*. Ed. J. T. Fraser. Amherst: University of Massachusetts Press, 1981.

Von Marten, Alfred. *Sociology of the Renaissance*. Trans. W. L. Luetkens. London: Kegan Paul, Trench, Trubner, 1944.

White, L. *Medieval Technology and Social Change*. Oxford: Clarendon, 1962.

Whitrow, G. J. *Time in History: Views of Time from Prehistory to the Present Day*. Oxford: Oxford University Press, 1989.

Whitson, Robley Edward. *The Coming Convergence of World Religions*. New York: Newman Press, 1971.

Wigoder, Geoffrey, ed. *Encyclopaedia Judaica*. Jerusalem: Encyclopaedia Judaica, 1994.

Wilcox, Donald J. *The Measure of Times Past: Pre-Newtonian Chronologies and the Rhetoric of Relative Time*. Chicago: University of Chicago Press, 1987.

Wissink, J. B. M. *The Eternity of the World in the Thought of Thomas Aquinas and His Contemporaries*. New York: E. J. Brill, 1990.

Zerubavel, Eviatar. *Hidden Rhythms: Schedules and Calendars in Social Life*. Chicago: University of Chicago Press, 1981.